The Beat Generation
A Beginner's Guide

T0105385

ONEWORLD BEGINNER'S GUIDES combine an original, inventive, and engaging approach with expert analysis on subjects ranging from art and history to religion and politics, and everything in between. Innovative and affordable, books in the series are perfect for anyone curious about the way the world works and the big ideas of our time.

anarchism
ruth kinna

anti-capitalism
simon tormey

artificial intelligence
blay whitby

the bahá'í faith
moojan momen

the beat generation
christopher gair

biodiversity
john spicer

bioterror & biowarfare
malcolm dando

the brain
a. al-chalabi, m. r. turner
& r. s. delamont

christianity
keith ward

cloning
aaron d. levine

criminal psychology
ray bull *et al.*

daoism
james miller

democracy
david beetham

energy
vaclav smil

evolution
burton s. guttman

evolutionary psychology
r. dunbar, l.barrett &
j. lycett

fair trade
jacqueline decarlo

genetics
a. griffiths, b.guttman,
d. suzuki & t. cullis

global terrorism
leonard weinberg

hinduism
klaus k. klostermaier

life in the universe
lewis dartnell

mafia & organized crime
james o. finckenauer

marx
andrew collier

NATO
jennifer medcalf

oil
vaclav smil

the palestine–israeli conflict
dan cohn-sherbok &
dawoud el-alami

paul
morna d. hooker

philosophy of mind
edward feser

postmodernism
kevin hart

quantum physics
alastair i. m. rae

religion
martin forward

the small arms trade
m. schroeder, r. stohl
& d. smith

sufism
william c. chittick

SELECTED FORTHCOMING TITLES:

astronomy	**feminism**	**modern slavery**
british politics	**globalization**	**philosophy of religion**
censorship	**history of science**	**political philosophy**
civil liberties	**humanism**	**psychology**
climate change	**journalism**	**racism**
crimes against humanity	**literary theory**	**renaissance art**
ethics	**middle east**	**romanticism**
existentialism	**medieval philosophy**	**socialism**

The Beat Generation
A Beginner's Guide

Christopher Gair

ONEWORLD

OXFORD

A Oneworld Book

First published by Oneworld Publications, 2008

ISBN 978–1–85168–542–4

Typeset by Jayvee, Trivandrum, India
Cover design by Two Associates
Printed and bound in the United States of America
by Thomson-Shore Inc.

Oneworld Publications
185 Banbury Road
Oxford OX2 7AR
England
www.oneworld-publications.com

Contents

Acknowledgements

It is appropriate that a book about the Beat Generation – a community of writers whose personal friendships were integral to their works – should also be indebted to the help of so many friends and colleagues. David Murray of the University of Nottingham was the first to advise me on the pitfalls inherent to transforming enthusiasm for the Beat Generation into scholarly discussion of them. Subsequently, colleagues at the University of Birmingham and fellow scholars who have devoted time to reading and responding to my work, or who have simply been there to discuss the Beat Generation, have provided invaluable support and inspiration. I am indebted to Scott Lucas, Jay Williams, Nick Selby, Ian Edwards, Sara Wood, Oliver Harris and Andy Green. Carolyn Cassady was gracious in her swift replies to early queries about the Beat Generation and in her support for my students when they too tapped her memories of Beat life. I am also grateful to Marina Vear, who sent me a copy of her dissertation on the British Beat Generation and helped to shape my thoughts on the international dimensions of the group.

I cannot put into words the debt that I owe Marsha Filion, my editor at Oneworld, who has continued to support this project throughout its over-lengthy gestation. As ever, my wife, Aliki, and children Juliette, Izzy and Dylan have also had to suffer while I involved them in the project. This book is dedicated to them.

Introduction

It is now (2007) fifty years since the publication of Jack Kerouac's *On the Road* and fifty-one since that of Allen Ginsberg's *Howl and Other Poems*. The anniversaries have been marked by a host of events, including interviews with surviving Beats, literary festivals, reassessments of classic texts, and plans for movie versions of *On the Road* and the life of Neal Cassady (the model for Dean Moriarty of *On the Road*). If anything, the central members of the Beat Generation are better known now than ever before, and it is evident that their legacy pervades many areas of American and global culture. The publication, with considerable fanfare, of *On the Road: The Original Scroll*, the text of the first version of the novel as typed by Kerouac onto a single roll of paper in 1951, to celebrate the half-century of its first issue, returns the book to the state that Kerouac intended, and the reception that it has received confirms that the Beat Generation won't be forgotten anytime soon.

'Howl' and *On the Road* were responsible for bringing the Beat Generation to the attention of a 'mainstream' audience for the first time and remain its best-known texts. Upon publication, *On the Road* was reviewed fairly widely, featured briefly on bestsellers lists and prompted the appearance of the thirty-five-year-old Kerouac on NBC's popular *The Tonight Show* with Steve Allen; although *Howl* was initially largely a local phenomenon in the San Francisco Bay region following Ginsberg's reading at the Six Gallery in October 1955, the obscenity trial that followed its release by Lawrence Ferlinghetti's City Lights publishing house provided the publicity necessary to generate national and international interest.

The media-shy Kerouac did his best to withdraw from public view – excepting a series of embarrassing drunken outbursts – and his other books generally sold poorly during the remainder of his life. In any case, his socially conservative views proved incompatible with the countercultural ideologies that superseded Beat thinking in the 1960s and at the time of his death in 1969 it appeared that his works would be remembered (if at all) as examples of a curious short-term event in American letters. Although *On the Road* never really disappeared from the must-read lists for would-be teenage rebels, it has only been in the past twenty-five years that Kerouac's other books have been consistently in print, previously unpublished materials have been released and his estate has become a multi-million-dollar industry whose ownership has been vigorously contested by his surviving relatives. In contrast, Ginsberg remained at the heart of countercultural movements throughout the 1960s and 1970s and was a significant poet (and much featured talking head) until his death in 1997.

The centrality of two writers and, specifically, of their respective most famous works has had significant ramifications in the manner that the Beat Generation has been remembered. First, because the books were published in the mid-1950s, in the middle of the Eisenhower presidencies, most readers tend to view the Beat Generation as a product of that time. In fact, many of the key players had met at or around the Columbia University campus in Manhattan a decade or more earlier and many of Kerouac's books, including *On the Road*, are set during the late 1940s and early 1950s. Kerouac himself made a distinction between two moments in Beat history: the first, 'a handful of really hip swinging cats' in the late 1940s, 'talking madly about that holy new feeling out there in the streets', whose brief moment 'vanished mighty swiftly during the Korean War . . . into jails and madhouses, or were shamed into silent conformity'; the second, 'the Korean post-war youth [that] emerged cool and beat, had picked up the gestures and the style, soon it was everywhere'.[1] Kerouac had written the majority of his major fiction between the publication of his first novel, *The Town and the City* (1950), and his second, *On the Road*, that is, in the period that separates his first and second Beat periods. Thus, apart from *The Dharma Bums* (1958), produced swiftly to cash in on *Road*'s success, Kerouac's novels published in the late 1950s and early 1960s had been drafted several years earlier. *On the Road* itself had a history stretching back almost a decade before its publication and was subjected to a series of rewritings before Kerouac was able to find a publisher willing to release it.

The success of *On the Road* and, to a lesser extent, *The Dharma Bums* has resulted in another distortion of Beat history. Because Kerouac's work has been so much more successful than that of any other novelist associated with the movement, his version of events has often been regarded as historical 'fact'. As several critics have recently reminded us, however, Kerouac's books are works of fiction, not autobiography, and the temptation to read them for their *strictly* historical veracity should be resisted. Apart from the rather obvious point that, as an insider participant–narrator, Kerouac (or his fictional alter egos such as Sal Paradise) has a vested interest in reporting particular versions of his adventures, it is also important to remember that (despite his participation in mid-century avant-garde experimentation) Kerouac was following a well-trodden path for American writers. *On the Road* and *The Dharma Bums*, for example, both repeat the 'classic' pattern of Herman Melville's *Moby-Dick* (1851) and F. Scott Fitzgerald's *The Great Gatsby* (1925) in their use of a participant-observer whose own

[1] Jack Kerouac, 'About the Beat Generation' (1957), in *The Portable Jack Kerouac*, edited by Ann Charters (New York: Penguin, 1996), pp. 559–60.

experiences are regarded as secondary to those of the central protagonists Ahab, Gatsby, Dean Moriarty and Japhy Ryder. As this link suggests, 'The Legend of Duluoz' (as Kerouac labelled the entirety of his autobiographical-fictional oeuvre) is a highly romanticized account that mythologizes real events within national archetypes.

A third consequence of the pre-eminence of Kerouac, Ginsberg and (to a slightly lesser extent) William Burroughs has been to give the impression that the Beat Generation was overwhelmingly the creation of a very few writers. There is an element of truth in this: the fact that so much of the movement's major work was produced by a handful of poets and novelists living outside the norms of middle-class American life should lead to a questioning of whether the epithet 'Generation' is a grandiose misnomer for a relatively small band. Ginsberg's tireless championing of his own friends' work, both before and after publication, has played a significant role in this process. Although he was later an impassioned promoter of other authors, his determination to see his own group's work in print and to promote it wherever possible contributed to the impression of a collective strategy even where individual writers were working to their own agendas. While there is no doubt, however, that Kerouac's and Burroughs's books have endured for reasons beyond Ginsberg's public relations skills, the effect has been to negate the importance of other participants. The Beat Generation – plus connected movements such as the San Francisco Renaissance – was a loose affiliation of artists with many different political and aesthetic agendas, and writers such as Diane di Prima, Gregory Corso, Lawrence Ferlinghetti and Gary Snyder (alongside many others) feature significantly in its history. It is also noteworthy that – despite his centrality as a presence within and mentor to others in the Beat Generation – almost all of Burroughs's major fiction was assembled and published well after the period usually associated with the Beat

Generation. It was only during his collaborations with the English artist, musician, writer and film-maker Brion Gysin in Paris in 1959 (as the 'Beat Generation' was being replaced by a media-hyped 'beatnik' industry that appalled Kerouac and other original Beats), that Burroughs developed the cut-up techniques that would characterize *Naked Lunch* (1959) and his subsequent works, and he lived in exile in Mexico, Tangier, Paris and London during the Beat Generation's most artistic and high-profile years, only returning to New York on a permanent basis in 1974. Novels such as *Naked Lunch* and *The Soft Machine* (1961) are in many ways far removed from the worlds represented by Kerouac or other Beats, and more closely resemble other experimental postmodernist fictions from the countercultural 1960s. As such, albeit reluctantly, I have omitted detailed readings of them from this book, which focuses on texts written during or directly about the Beat world of the 1940s and 1950s.

The range and diversity of Beat literary production has been an important factor in constructing a narrative of the 'Beat Generation'. Although it is not hard to make aesthetic links between, for example, Kerouac and Ginsberg, or to identify the influence of both writers on second-generation Beats such as Bob Dylan, attempts at wider definitions rapidly become problematic. Given the willingness of Kerouac and many other male Beats to adopt patriarchal values, even when challenging other aspects of American life, how can the proto-feminism of much Beat writing by women be situated as part of the same literary genre? Indeed, is such an approach desirable when it could be argued that the Beat Generation was more of a social than a literary 'movement', its bases in New York and San Francisco serving as artistic retreats for young people sharing a sense of alienation from the values dominant in post-war America, but pursuing a range of artistic ambitions? Perhaps it would be better to adapt James Freeman Clark's classification of the Transcendentalists as 'a club of the likeminded, I suppose, because no two of us thought alike'[2] as an equally apposite definition of a group that was, in many ways, the Transcendentalists' literary and cultural descendant.

TRANSCENDENTALISM

The Transcendentalists were a loose affiliation of philosophers and poets largely based in New England and New York, who were most prominent between the 1830s and 1850s. Leading figures included Ralph Waldo Emerson (1803–82), Margaret Fuller (1810–50), Henry David Thoreau (1817–62), Walt Whitman (1819–92) and Amos Bronson Alcott (1799–1888), while the American novelists Nathaniel Hawthorne (1804–64) and Herman Melville (1819–91) were somewhat sceptical fellow-travellers. Emerson's philosophy – often filtered through Whitman or Thoreau – is a key component of much Beat thinking. In essays such as 'Nature' (1836), 'Self-Reliance' (1841) and 'The American Scholar' (1837), Emerson argued that humankind had become over-civilized and increasingly covetous of material goods. An over-reliance on book knowledge and a fear of non-conformity were (for the Transcendentalists) the signs of a community in which economic comfort had become a goal that was destroying the human spirit. Emerson's celebration of aboriginal, 'primitive' cultures as vibrant alternatives to white America anticipated Kerouac's often naive and embarrassing representations of the African American or Mexican as an idealized counter to Eisenhower-era suburbia.

Emerson's response to conformity was to insist on the importance of spontaneity and self-trust. In a precursor to Kerouac and Ginsberg's mantra, 'First thought, best thought,' he insisted that it was essential that the poet listen to his (sic) 'Reason', a concept

[2] Quoted by Michael Meyer in his introduction to Henry David Thoreau, *Walden and Civil Disobedience* (Harmondsworth, England: Penguin, 1983), p. 9.

TRANSCENDENTALISM (*cont.*)

that demanded a transcendental refusal to allow the mind to be constrained by cultural norms. Reason provided a form of access to the Absolute and it is unsurprising that the Transcendentalists looked to nature as the best guide to how the human mind could arrive at an order that moved beyond the artificialities of what they perceived to be stifling modernity. While Transcendentalism owed a large ideological debt to Kantian philosophy and British Romanticism, its celebration of the possibilities offered by the vast expanses of the American landscape led to the belief that European idealism could be brought to fruition in a United States that would turn to its poets for spiritual leadership. Alongside Emerson's essays, the most significant Transcendentalist works for the Beat Generation were *Walden* (1854), Thoreau's account of his time living in a cabin next to Walden Pond, which influenced both Kerouac and Gary Snyder, and Whitman's *Leaves of Grass* (1855–1892), a repeatedly revised and expanded poetic representation of the United States, whose free verse style was the basis for 'Howl' and many of Ginsberg's other poems. Ginsberg's 'A Supermarket in California' (1955) acknowledges the debt, imagining Whitman transplanted to the West Coast of the 1950s.

It is hard to identify a manifesto shared by all Transcendentalists, since, like the Beat Generation a century later, their insistence on spontaneous free thinking encouraged differences of opinion. It is, however, possible to identify two camps that also anticipate Beat politics: on the one hand, Emerson and Thoreau were examples of the sort of individualism increasingly championed by Kerouac as an antidote to the standardization he observed in mid-twentieth-century America. On the other hand, collective farming experiments such as George Ripley's Brook Farm (1841–7; parodied in Hawthorne's novel, *The Blithedale Romance* [1852]) and Bronson Alcott and Charles Lane's *Fruitlands* (1843–4) provided models for the often equally chaotic communal retreats that would characterize much countercultural practice in the 1950s and 1960s.

The above should provide some clues to the aims of this book. In it, I will provide an introduction to the history, reception and legacy of the 'Beat Generation' which draws upon but also challenges the established narratives. Studies of the Beat Generation have tended to do one of two things: on the one hand, early works focused on Kerouac's *On the Road* (1957) and Ginsberg's *Howl and Other Poems* (1956) to the exclusion not only of other writers, but also of other works by Kerouac and Ginsberg. Where this kind of analysis does stray beyond *On The Road* and *Howl*, its scope remains narrow – generally adding Gregory Corso and William Burroughs to the Beat 'canon' and discussing seminal events such as the Six Gallery reading where Ginsberg performed 'Howl' alongside readings by other Beat poets, but leaving the central tenets of what it meant to be 'Beat' unchallenged. More recent studies have questioned these narratives, noting the presence of women writers as well as the often-overlooked ethnic mix of figures associated with Beat. In general, however, these readings, have extended inclusiveness at the expense of a dilution of what it meant to be Beat and via over-critical attacks on Kerouac and – to a lesser extent – Ginsberg. While there have been recent approaches that have provided welcome rejoinders to the mythologizing tendencies of the Beat Generation and their early critics, there is still no coherent overview of this movement.

The Beat Generation: A Beginner's Guide aims to rectify the problems inherent to earlier studies, providing a clear historical narrative that chronicles the inner workings of the Beat movement. The book will look at issues of influences, origins and legacies, combining (brief) biographical accounts of the leading players with readings of selective texts within a history of Beat life. It seems self-evident that, half a century after the publication of *Howl* and *On the Road*, the Beat Generation continue to attract new readers in large numbers. While one reason for this is the extent to which their work has been incorporated by a 'mainstream' popular culture that now uses *On the Road* to sell jeans and parodies 'Howl' in *The Simpsons*, *The Beat Generation* will also stress the extent to which works by Beat writers are now regarded as significant contributions to the American literary canon as well as offering models of freedom and resistance to dominant structures that still appeal to new readers today.

1

Challenging 'America': Reinventing the arts in the 1940s

In this chapter, I will set the scene for the emergence of the 'Beat Generation'. First, I will chart the cultural context – post-1945 American society – within which the Beat Generation emerged, noting not only the causes of alienation at the time – most significantly, a culture of consumption that invited conformity alongside restrictive sexual mores that indicated intolerance of transgression – but also the extent to which many 'ordinary' Americans found these values repressive. Thus, I will point out that while the Beat Generation's ways of expressing alienation were often startlingly different from the norms of wider culture, the sense of alienation itself was much more widespread than would be imagined from glances at how 'America' generally represented itself at the time.

Any narrative considering the range of locations in which the Beat Generation sought alternatives to post-war America is inevitably diverse. Their range of influences will necessitate – at different stages in this book – glances back to British Romanticism (in particular, William Blake), American Transcendentalism (especially Walt Whitman) and earlier twentieth-century American writers such as William Carlos Williams, Henry Miller and Thomas Wolfe, but in this chapter I will assess the degree to which the Beat Generation drew on contemporaneous figures in other genres, such as Charlie

Parker/Bebop, Marlon Brando/Method Acting and Jackson Pollock/Abstract Expressionism. I take time in the following pages to assess the significance of the arts of the 1940s as models for the emerging Beat Generation. By resituating the Beat Generation within these historical contexts, I will undertake a reassessment of the romanticized narrative that has grown around the Beat Generation, challenging this story in a number of ways.

The United States at mid-century

Histories of the Beat Generation tend to be constructed around a handful of 'pivotal' encounters and incidents: the first meeting between Kerouac and Ginsberg at Columbia in 1944 and the establishment of a small community also including William Burroughs, Lucien Carr, Hal Chase, Edie Parker and Joan Vollmer; the killing of David Kammerer by Carr; the introduction of Neal Cassady to this group and the intense effect that he had on Kerouac and Ginsberg; the shooting of Vollmer by Burroughs in Mexico in 1951 and Burroughs's subsequent confession, 'I am forced to the appalling conclusion that I would have never become a writer but for Joan's death . . . The death of Joan brought me into contact with the invader, the Ugly Spirit, and maneuvered me into a lifelong struggle, in which I had no choice except to write my way out';[1] the night at the Six Gallery in San Francisco in October 1955 when Ginsberg performed 'Howl' for the first time and Gary Snyder, Michael McClure, Philip Lamantia and Philip Whalen also read; Kerouac and Cassady's road trips across America; and the decline and early death of Kerouac.

---

[1] William S. Burroughs, *Queer* (New York: Viking, 1985), p. xxii.

While there is no doubt that each of these incidents is of immense importance in the shaping of the Beat Generation, and I will discuss many of them in detail later in this book, there are also dangers in focusing on them too narrowly and forgetting the wider context within which they occurred. The America of the mid-1940s was a place of rapid political and cultural transition: the Depression of the 1930s, which had shaped the childhoods of most of the Beat Generation, had been superseded by American involvement in the Second World War and by the atomic bombings of Hiroshima and Nagasaki in August 1945, events that (among other things) had a profound effect on the counter-culture of the following years. Domestically, the post-war era was marked by rapid improvement in economic conditions, by the emergence of what President Dwight D. Eisenhower would later (in his 1961 Farewell Address) label the 'military-industrial complex', by the birth of the 'baby boomer' generation that would invent an entirely new form of youth culture in the following two decades, and by the re-adoption of a culture of consumption (echoing both the 1890s and the 1920s) that encouraged the rapid standardization of family life and celebrated the belief that the nation was entering a golden age in which science would offer increased leisure and luxury for all.

Within the general mood of economic confidence, there are several points that stand out. First, it is important to stress the links between the technological and ideological components of cultural change. With post-war prosperity, many Americans were able to take advantage of relatively new inventions such as the automobile, television and refrigerator and to move to large suburban homes where they pursued lifestyles unimaginable during the Depression. While some sociologists perceived threats to the sense of social cohesion or community in these large-scale relocations, the fact that viewing options were limited to a few channels whose output was largely determined by the need to satisfy corporate advertisers meant that viewer choice was strictly limited. Even if adults were no longer going out to the movies in anything like pre-war numbers, large numbers of Americans were watching the same shows and discussing them at work or school or home the next day, contributing to a sense of social cohesion and – more sinisterly – enabling the state–corporate system to maintain a form of 'soft' supervision of its citizens. The era in which the Beat Generation came to artistic maturity was, of course, the height of the Cold War, and the need to promise material success to loyal American citizens was integral to governmental efforts to demonstrate the nation's 'superiority' to the Soviet Union both to its own citizens and to the rest of the world. While there were many Americans who were excluded from the model of suburban affluence (most notably, a high proportion of African Americans), what sociologist C. Wright Mills labelled the 'Power Elite' in the United States were remarkably adept in controlling the version of the nation that was represented in movies and television programmes.

The counter to the economic rewards for loyalty to American Cold War ideology was an intolerance of even the suspicion of political dissidence. Most famously, the Wisconsin Senator Joseph McCarthy led a campaign of intimidation that resulted in the 'outing' of hundreds of individuals with real or alleged ties to communism. The House Un-American Activities Commission (HUAC) and the Senate Permanent Subcommittee on Investigations, as well as the FBI, headed by the passionately anti-communist (and, later, anti-beatnik) J. Edgar Hoover, all campaigned against not only workers in political institutions, but also against anyone in the arts and media who was perceived to be left-leaning. Stephen Vaughn has noted, for example, the 'virtual impossibility of bringing an openly anticapitalist picture to the screen', since the studio system excluded writers offering well-disposed representations of radical causes. Even when such a movie was made, its distribution would be stymied. Thus, for example, Herbert Biberman's *Salt of the Earth* (1954), a sympathetic and accurate portrayal of working-class life in the United States, was delayed while Biberman was imprisoned (following a HUAC investigation) and, despite winning numerous awards in Europe, only received proper national distribution in 1965.[2] Ironically, Hoover would even identify the Beat Generation as a threat to American society, despite the fact that many, including Kerouac, were social conservatives who chose to live outside mainstream America rather than attempting to convert it.

Dissonant voices: Acting, music, painting

Despite the kind of conformity increasingly demanded by state and corporate authority, resistance surfaced in a variety of places. The 1940s were an age of great artistic innovation and the challenges to the orthodoxies of the previous decade – for example, Bebop's dismantling of the structures of Swing in jazz and Abstract Expressionism's emergence as a counter to the social realism of the 1930s in painting – offer indications of the zeitgeist that would shape the ideology of the early Beat Generation. Likewise, Marlon Brando's portrayal of Stanley Kowalski in the 1947 Broadway production of Tennessee Williams's *A Streetcar Named Desire* indicated a move in the arts towards establishing the primacy of the gesture and of unmediated passion above the traditional stress on clarity of verbal expression.

---

[2] See Stephen Vaughn, 'Political Censorship during the Cold War: The Hollywood Ten', in *Movie Censorship and American Culture*, edited by Francis G. Couvares (Washington and London: Smithsonian Institution Press, 1996), p. 246.

MARLON BRANDO

Marlon Brando (1924–2004) was in many ways the archetype of the Beat-made-good. After his father abandoned the family, Brando experienced a nomadic childhood, travelling with his alcoholic mother and siblings through Depression-era Nebraska, California and Illinois. While this early life bears resemblance to that of Beat icon Neal Cassady, Brando's youth also has an uncanny similarity to that of William Burroughs, Brando's dispatch to the Shattuck Military Academy in Minnesota seeming remarkably akin to Burrough's relocation to the Los Alamos Ranch School in New Mexico, in both cases after being perceived as a troublemaker at school. While the Academy did appear to stimulate Brando's long-held interest in acting, it was also the scene of further insubordination (a Kerouacesque refusal to obey orders from officers) and he dropped out of school. By the early 1940s, Brando had moved to New York and combined hanging out in Greenwich Village with studying acting at the New School's Dramatic Workshop, where he practised the Stanislavski system, in which the actor was encouraged to identify as closely as possible with his or her role in order to bring it to life. The system demanded that actors imagine what their character would do in a range of different situations in order that their stage performances would convey a sense of authenticity. Great stress was laid on the significance of physical action, with an actor using the limitless possibilities of his or her body as the primary means of communicating with the audience.

Brando's 1947 stage performance as Stanley Kowalski in *A Streetcar Named Desire* virtually single-handedly effected a revolution in American stage and screen acting, and led to the emergence of Method Acting as the dominant form of the 1950s and beyond. Brando himself swiftly adapted his stage success to screen roles, including Elia Kazan's 1951 version of *Streetcar*. Brando's role as biker gang leader Johnny Stabler in Laslo Benedek's *The Wild One* (1953) was instrumental in establishing the image of alienated youth that would be so significant in American popular culture in the 1950s. When Johnny is asked,

MARLON BRANDO (*cont.*)

'What are you rebelling against?' and replies, 'What've you got?' he articulates the sense of total alienation from mainstream culture that would reside at the heart not only of the Beat desire to move beyond the 'Plastic Fifties', but also called out to James Dean, Elvis Presley and a generation of teenage baby boomers about to come of age as a new counterculture.

Brando's early parts are characterized by the establishment of a screen persona that transcends individual roles. Brando was – on screen and in his early life – a kind of spiritual brother to Neal Cassady (or, better, the Dean Moriarty of Kerouac's imagination in *On the Road*), representing an untameable force of nature that refuses to cooperate with or correspond to the demands of white mainstream American life. Like Moriarty, he seemed to be particularly threatening to this world because of his appeal to sexually repressed women (Kathie Bleeker in *The Wild One*, Camille in *On the Road*) who had been denied any kind of expression of their latent passions in their own communities.

The birth of bebop

Bebop – and especially the alto saxophonist Charlie 'Bird' Parker – became pivotal to Kerouac's ideas on improvisation and spontaneity of composition, and provided him with a model for his own work. Jazz of the 1930s had been dominated by Swing, a form that established jazz as the most popular musical genre in the decade. Swing was performed by relatively large bands, many led by household names such as Count Basie, Duke Ellington, Benny Goodman, Artie Shaw and Cab Calloway. It was characterized by tight structures and arrangements and by the emergence of star soloists such as saxophonist Lester Young (an early hero of Kerouac's) and trumpeter Roy Eldridge. With the United States' entry into the Second World War, Swing's popularity waned for a number of reasons: many of the band members were conscripted into the military; it became increasingly uneconomic to go on the road with such large numbers of musicians; taxes on dance halls were introduced or increased. Most importantly, however, a new generation of musicians became frustrated with the constraints imposed by Swing arrangements and sought new ways of playing. The early Beboppers – including, most notably, Parker, Dizzy Gillespie, Charlie Christian and Thelonius Monk – would gather in clubs such as Minton's in Harlem to play a new music that was characterized by small groups jamming on what were then unusual chord changes and harmonic arrangements over complex rhythmic patterns that seemed remote from the dance-friendly rhythms of Swing. Most importantly, Bebop created a collective environment in which improvisation was the norm not just for a featured soloist, but for the whole group. The music demanded high levels of technical competence and anyone who could not meet the high standards expected by the crowd at Minton's would soon be removed: as trumpeter Miles Davis recollected, 'You had to put up or shut up, there was no in between.'[3]

Bebop clearly offered a model for the compositional philosophy of Beats such as Kerouac and Ginsburg. Its coupling of the need for expert knowledge of earlier musical forms and a technical mastery based upon years of practice that would enable performance of highly complex pieces to appear 'spontaneous' is self-evidently mirrored in Kerouac's habit of spending hours 'sketching', or writing descriptions of what he saw from a window or coffee shop in preparation for the 'spontaneous prose' of his novels. Of equal significance was Bebop's liminal position on the border of the black and white worlds of Harlem and the lower Manhattan of 52nd Street, or simply 'The Street'. Although Kerouac and others did travel to Harlem to hear the music, its

---

[3] Miles Davis with Quincy Troupe, *Miles: The Autobiography* (London: Picador, 1990), p. 44.

presence so close to home also exposed them to an African American culture and language that would have a profound (if misunderstood and romanticized) effect on their own work.

The lifestyles of figures such as Parker also served as models for the Beat Generation. While it was possible to share Miles Davis's opinion of Parker's insatiable appetite for drugs, alcohol, women and food as sheer greed, Parker's life also represented a defiant refusal to conform to white expectations. Kerouac, in particular, felt a close affinity with Parker (see chapter 4), devoting a lengthy passage to a description of him in *The Subterraneans*. In the early days in New York before Kerouac went on the road, jazz and its players showed him an alternative to the worlds he had known as a boy in white working-class Lowell and later at the bastions of privilege, Horace Mann prep school and Columbia, and even to his experiences at sea.

Abstract expressionism

While bop was indubitably the most significant of the local, contemporary artistic developments to aid in the shaping of a proto-Beat culture in New York in the 1940s, it was not the only one. Strikingly similar transformations were occurring in painting, with the social realism of the Depression years replaced by Abstract Expressionism – or Action Painting – in which the artist became as significant as his (sic) canvas. Again, this was very much a New York movement that, along with occurrences in theatre and music, illustrated the extent to which this metropolis had replaced Paris and other 'Old World' cities as the centre of the artistic world. In some ways, the connections between painters and Beats were personal: many would drink together in Greenwich Village's Cedar Tavern and the Waldorf Cafeteria and when Willem de Kooning transformed a New York factory loft into a living space he anticipated a move that would be re-enacted by innumerable Beats in the 1950s.

More importantly, however, the Abstract Expressionism of the 1940s and 1950s provides yet another example of the degree to which Beat ideas about composition were already widely shared within the New York artistic avant-garde in the years immediately preceding the publication of the Beat Generation's first major works. Although the styles of the 'essential eight' Abstract Expressionists – Jackson Pollock, Willem de Kooning, Barnett Newman, Ad Reinhardt, Clyfford Still, Adolph Gottlieb, Robert Motherwell and Mark Rothko – were as diverse as those of the central Beat writers, their work can be categorized in ways that offer useful parallels. First, many of the artists shared the belief, put forward by Clement Greenberg, the principal theorist of Abstract Expressionism, that 'expression [matters] more than what is being expressed'. For artists such as Pollock, this meant that all attempts at representational art should be abandoned: in their place, the artist should emphasize his (sic) immersion in the act of painting itself, creating (often vast) works celebrating the possibilities of linear complexity and the relationship between colours.[4] Again, we could jump ahead here to Kerouac's fiction – in particular, to novels such as *The Subterraneans* and *Visions of Cody* – to witness the same effect at work in his use of words, where rhythmic patterns and collations are afforded more significance than direct communication of 'meaning'. The Abstract Expressionist emphasis on the work of art as a unique object in a world of mass reproduction and standardization also corresponds closely with the Beat Generation's own desire to generate literature that transcended the consumption-obsessed world that surrounded them. Antipathy to the world around them encouraged the artists to create texts that make no effort to represent that world and

[4] See Clement Greenberg, 'Avant-Garde and Kitsch', in *Partisan Review*, 6.5 (1939), pp. 34–49, reprinted in Francis Frascina (ed.), *Pollock and After: The Critical Debate*, 2nd edn (London and New York: Routledge, 2000), pp. 48–59, especially p. 50.

attempt to imagine the work of art as a world in itself. Although, ironically, much Abstract Expressionist art (and, decades later, original Beat manuscripts) would change hands for millions of dollars as part of the market economy they strived to subvert or escape, both groups aimed to produce examples of a genuine culture that they feared was being destroyed by the kitsch mass culture of quiz shows and soap operas.

JACKSON POLLOCK

Jackson Pollock (1912–56) is now considered to be one of the United States' greatest painters and was the most famous of the Abstract Expressionists, becoming the first 'art star' in America and appearing as often in the gossip columns as in arts journals. Born in Cody, Wyoming in 1912, Pollock spent his childhood in Arizona and California. In 1930, he moved to New York to study with the regionalist painter Thomas Hart Benton at the Art Students League. Pollock spent three years with Benton, learning conventional techniques and developing his own early style, combining themes drawn from the west of his childhood with Benton's swirling approach to the representation of nature. By the mid-1930s, Pollock was starting to discover the abstract style that would make him famous and drew on sources such as Native American sandpainting and the Mexican muralists, as well as European Surrealism and Cubism and modernist theories about stream-of-consciousness creativity, in the search for his own voice. Pollock married Lee Krasner in 1945 and moved to a farmhouse in Long Island where he painted his best-known works. The location offered a combination of inspirational landscapes and the space to develop his characteristic large canvasses. Many of these works were composed with the canvas pinned to the ground. Pollock would walk around it, splashing paint in a physically active manner far from the conventional notion of the artist standing at an easel, and was labelled 'Jack the Dripper' by *Time* magazine. Although Pollock earned relatively little from sales of his paintings,

JACKSON POLLOCK (*cont.*)

they have been purchased for enormous sums in recent years. *Number 5, 1948* was sold for US$140,000,000 in 2006.

Pollock's life was marked by his alcoholism and he died drunk at the wheel in a car crash in 1956. His death – coming a year after those of Charlie Parker and James Dean – ensured that he would become a member of the live-fast, die-young fraternity mythologized by the emergent counterculture and later to include both Jack Kerouac and Neal Cassady. His lifestyle, especially after he became famous following a 1949 feature in *Life* magazine, bears considerable resemblance to that of Kerouac after the publication of *On the Road*. More significant are the strong similarities between the aesthetic beliefs and compositional practices of Pollock and Kerouac. There is evidence to suggest that Kerouac's spontaneous prose was inspired in part by Pollock's work, and artist and writer shared the then widespread artistic emphasis on the primacy of direct gestures. Both imagined the work of art as a unique production that stood apart from the mass-produced goods that dominated American life, but, whereas most critics and mainstream politicians were overtly hostile to the Beat Generation, Pollock – and Abstract Expressionism more generally – was swiftly adopted by the artistic and political establishments as an embodiment of the American freedom and individualism that contrasted sharply with a perceived lack of these qualities in the Soviet Union. Likewise, while Kerouac was spending his most creative years (the early 1950s) alternating between life with his mother and subsistence-level travels with a rucksack of unpublished manuscripts, Pollock enjoyed the patronage of Peggy Guggenheim, which guaranteed both a regular income and regular one-man shows in her New York gallery, Art of this Century, which opened in 1941 and exhibited Pollock in 1943, 1945 and 1947. Much has been made of the fact that Pollock liked to listen to jazz while he worked, although his tastes veered more to older forms than to Bebop. He was, however, recognized as one of the like-minded by the more avant-garde end of the jazz community of the 1950s and a reproduction of one of his paintings was used for the cover of saxophonist Ornette Coleman's *Free Jazz* (1960).

Teenage kicks: Rock and roll and juvenile alienation

Events outlined above suggest a fortuitous synchronicity not only in the convergence of Jack Kerouac, William Burroughs, Lucien Carr, Allen Ginsberg et al. around the Columbia campus in 1943–4 but also in their arrival at the very moment when so much was occurring within the Manhattan artistic community which would prove conducive to their own fledgling ideas. While – as we shall see in the chapters that follow – many literary figures from the nineteenth century would inspire the group of young would-be writers, the emerging Beat manifesto of the ensuing decade can only be truly comprehended within the revolutionary artistic environment of the New York of the mid-1940s to the mid-1950s.

But what of the nation beyond the small communities of musicians, painters, actors and writers who were imagining new ways of looking at the world? What happened in America during the 1950s to create a situation in which the preachings of a small group of artists (hardly, when Kerouac and John Clellon Holmes first came up with the term, a Beat *Generation* at all) reached out to attract large numbers of young Americans and create the beatnik phenomenon at the end of the decade?

As I have already suggested, one factor in the transformation of American culture in the 1950s and 1960s was demographic. The post-war baby boom, running approximately from 1945 to 1961, created an enormous market of young consumers eager to develop their own forms of popular and niche culture that would differ greatly from those of their parents' generation. While conservative critics were swift to condemn the teen culture of the mid-1950s as nothing more than an epidemic of juvenile delinquency, the youth culture of the time was manifested in a range of significant ways. In addition to the emergence of the beatnik, we could think of the re-invention of Rhythm and Blues – essentially a form played and listened to by African Americans – as Rock and Roll, a craze that, especially with the arrival of Elvis Presley, swept away the crooners who had dominated the charts until then and replaced them with 'wild' performers such as Jerry Lee Lewis, Little Richard and Eddie Cochran. To illustrate the rapid transformation of youth culture at this time, it is worth remembering that the (for many) archetypal teen film of the 1950s, Nicholas Ray's *Rebel without a Cause* (1955), starring James Dean – who died in an automobile accident shortly before its release – is accompanied by a jazz soundtrack that would rapidly seem anachronistic with the release of Elvis's first single, 'That's All Right' (1954), and the 'juvenile delinquent' movie *The Blackboard Jungle* (1955), at the start of which Bill Haley and the Comets' 'Rock Around the Clock' plays over the credits.

Rock and Roll was indicative of the gulf between 1950s teenagers and their parents. While the latter had grown up during the Depression of the 1930s and were now generally delighted to enjoy the material comforts provided by a post-war economic boom that delivered suburbia, refrigerators and televisions to broad swathes of the white population, their children were less easily satisfied. Of course, financial security filtered through to teens who were able to listen to the new music in their bedrooms and borrow their parents' cars, but this did not seem like enough. Kerouac's promise of joy, kicks, freedom and adventure on the open road offered a spectacularly romantic alternative to Rock Hudson and Doris Day or the television diet of quiz shows and domestic sit-coms. Beat language, with its phraseology drawn from the hip African American jazz talk of urban streets – at least, as imagined by Beats and their new devotees – offered an antidote to the sterility of a culture in which young middle-class boys were expected to grow up and become lawyers or doctors and their sisters expected to marry young and have four or five kids of their own. There was thus a ready-made market eager to digest books articulating youthful alienation and transform intensely personal experiences into a kind of cultural manifesto challenging the beliefs cherished by an older generation of Americans.

For Kerouac, Ginsberg and many other first-generation Beats, however, the kids were missing the point. Kerouac saw the 'beatific' in Beat – an ideology with the spiritual at its heart – and was appalled at the manner in which his vision was transformed into the latest commodity. Ginsberg, too, while more attuned to the possibilities for social change that could stem from the mass mobilization of young people against the culture of abundance that seemed to shape the Eisenhower years, was clearly concerned at the speed with which so many young people embraced beatnik identities. He spent most of the late 1950s and early 1960s in exile, living in Paris and travelling (often with his lover, Peter Orlovsky) in South America, North Africa, Europe and India. Likewise, William Burroughs spent little of this time in the United States, remaining in Tangier for several years before moving to Paris and London.

In order to understand the ambivalence – or even outright hostility – expressed by the Beat Generation at a moment when they could have been cherishing the success that they had dreamed of for so long, it is necessary to step back a decade or more to a time when a group of young men and women met one another in the generally rather staid environs of prestigious Columbia University. There, they felt that they were among the last few protectors (at least, within the privileged, sanitized white world they inhabited) of a belief in the primacy of art in experiencing life. While they could look to earlier European and American writers and to other cultures such as that of the hipster-addicts congregating around Times Square or the urban African American world that was generating a music and an argot that could help them to express their own sentiments, they had no texts to match those that they would later produce for the next generation of alienated youths, who would find an apparently ready-made expression of their own angst in the works of Ginsberg and Kerouac.

2

The birth of Beat

The Beat Generation tends to be remembered as a product of and reaction against the stifling conformity of the Eisenhower presidency of the 1950s. Nevertheless, while it was only after the success of *On the Road* in 1957–8 that Beat became beatnik and its leading figures became nationally and internationally known, they had met and produced a loose artistic manifesto more than a decade earlier. The first gathering of Jack Kerouac, Allen Ginsberg, William Burroughs, Lucien Carr, Joan Vollmer, Edie Parker and Céline Young – the original 'Beat' circle – occurred on and around the Columbia campus in spring 1944 and the (often very different) visions of a small group of would-be writers helped to construct the beginnings of a 'movement'. Burroughs met the Times Square hustler Herbert Huncke (rhyming with 'junkie') the same year and swiftly introduced him to Ginsberg and Kerouac, thus exposing them to an important version of 'Beat'. Neal Cassady – the model for the legendary Dean Moriarty of *On the Road* – arrived in New York for the first time in December 1946, travelling across the country in a Greyhound bus with his teenage wife LuAnne Henderson and was introduced to Ginsberg and Kerouac by Hal Chase, a Columbia anthropology student from Denver, Cassady's home town. John Clellon Holmes, author of *Go*, the 'first' Beat novel, and credited as co-creator (along with Kerouac) of the moniker 'Beat Generation' became a peripheral member of the scene from 1948, but – as *Go* suggests – was always too 'square' to become fully involved and stayed in the city when Kerouac took to the road with Cassady. Ginsberg encountered Carl Solomon in the Psychiatric Institute in New York in 1949 and used many of the phrases uttered by Solomon as he recovered from electric shock treatment in 'Howl for Carl Solomon', the poem that made him famous. Ginsberg met Gregory Corso, the juvenile delinquent poet rebel in a Greenwich Village bar in 1950, thus completing the coming together of the most significant of the first generation of East Coast Beats.

In this chapter, I outline the central figures and events from the early days of the Beat Generation in New York City and on the road until Ginsberg relocated to San Francisco in 1954. I stress the extent to which – from the very start – the Beat Generation saw themselves as serious artists, immersed in canonical and avant-garde materials and attempting a revolution in American literature, even at a time when little of their work had been published outside small college magazines. This dedication was integral to their subsequent success but was also an aspect of their identity that (after the success of *On the Road*) was ridiculed by conservative literary culture and ignored by a popular press eager to parody Beat as beatnik.

Jack Kerouac

Jean Louis Lebris de Kerouac (1922–69) was born and raised in the industrial town of Lowell, Massachusetts. The son of joual-speaking French Canadian immigrants, he came from a solidly working-class background. His father was a printer and journalist, fond of socializing and playing the horses, and his mother worked in a shoe factory, but they shared the quintessential immigrant faith in social advancement through education and hard work.

Leo Kerouac and Gabrielle L'Evesque had been born in Quebec and migrated to the United States as children. After leaving school, Leo Kerouac trained as a journalist and typesetter on a local French-language paper and met and married

Gabrielle, who spent her early adulthood working in a shoe factory. The couple settled in a French-speaking district of Lowell, an industrial New England town largely populated by a combination of French Canadian, Greek, Irish and Polish settlers. Kerouac recounted his parents' early careers in detail in his first published novel, *The Town and the City* (1950), and chronicles the inter-ethnic friendships that he formed in Lowell in his series of Lowell novels that fictionalize his own youth before his departure for New York. Significantly, there was no black community in Lowell, a point highlighted by Kerouac in his description of an athletic encounter with a 'Negro' sprinter in *Maggie Cassidy* and an absence that helps to explain the conflicted and often ill-informed opinions about African Americans that recur throughout his oeuvre.

Leo and Gabrielle had three children: Gerard, born in 1916; Caroline, in 1918; and Jack. Gerard, in particular, played a profound role in shaping Jack's future life, although he died of rheumatic fever age nine when Jack was only four. After his death, Gerard was viewed as a saint by the local nuns and idealized by his mother, who repeatedly let Jack know that the wrong son had been allowed to live. While this helps to explain Kerouac's insecurity, his unusual relationship with his mother and his fear that anyone he loved would be taken from him, Gerard's influence is also evident in more positive ways, such as in a passionate love for animals and in a desire to explore and understand the world which was driven by religious curiosity.

Strangely, for a man who would find fame through his use of American vernacular, Kerouac did not speak English for the first several years of his childhood and continued to regard it as a second language until after his arrival in New York in his late teens. Throughout his life, he was proud of his French ancestry (which he claimed to be aristocratic) and regularly inserted French phrases into his prose. It was, therefore, a shock to Kerouac that when he finally spent time in Paris in his forties, expecting to be greeted as a long-lost brother, the locals mocked his provincial accent and (to them) unsophisticated ways. Nevertheless, this heritage is essential to an understanding of Kerouac's take on America. As an outsider (by language and as a result of his French Canadian parents), there seems to be a combination of fascination and repulsion in his view of America. Seymour Krim suggests that for Kerouac, as a first-generation immigrant, 'the history and raw beauty of the U.S. legend was more crucially important than it was to the comparatively well-adjusted runnynoses who took their cokes and movies for granted and fatly basked in the swarm of American customs . . . that young Kerouac made into his interior theatricals'.[1]

Like William Burroughs, Kerouac took an early interest in writing, composing fiction and poetry, and – in a precursor of his later practice of transforming his life into words – inventng supernatural fantasies that combined the realities of life in Lowell with an escapism drawing upon movies, comics and radio shows. Importantly, even in his youth in Lowell, Kerouac regarded literature not just as a solitary occupation but also as the basis for friendship and debate with boys including Sebastian 'Sammy' Sampas, Cornelius 'Connie' Murphy, Ed Tully and John MacDonald. The result was that Kerouac was well primed to articulate his own sense of the supreme importance of literature to humankind by the time he moved to New York in his teens, and was aware that even in a small working-class community such as Lowell there were like-minded people. Therefore, although there were of course major changes to his life from the moment that he arrived in the city, there were also aspects of his encounter with the proto-Beat group that would seem familiar.

[1] Seymour Krim, introduction to Jack Kerouac, *Desolation Angels* (London: Granada, 1972), p. 11.

Kerouac is discussed in detail in chapter 4, but it is worth stressing one further point at this stage. In addition to his literary talents, Kerouac was also an outstanding athlete, who arrived at the exclusive Horace Mann School in 1939 and moved to Columbia in September 1940 on a football scholarship. In Lowell, he moved between his track and literary friends and their respective cultures and continued to do the same in New York, and the contrast between his 'jock' exterior and sensitivity to poetry proved to be a surprise to new literary acquaintances. Although not tall, Kerouac had an imposing physical presence that, coupled with his good looks and tendency towards moodiness, made him attractive to many women. This physicality marks Kerouac as very different in appearance from, in particular, Allen Ginsberg and William Burroughs, but aligns him with Neal Cassady, another fine athlete (and a figure even more desirable for many women than Kerouac himself) in an element of Beat identity celebrating the physical possibilities (sporting as well as sexual) of the body.

By the time that Kerouac met Carr, Ginsberg and the other proto-Beats, he had already raised and dashed his parents' hopes that he would enact their vision of the American Dream. He quickly became disillusioned with both the academic and sporting environments that he entered at Columbia and began to explore and enjoy the other pleasures offered by New York. Following a fall-out with his football coach, a broken leg, and failure in some courses, he abandoned his degree, a step that his father found hard to understand or forgive. With hindsight, it is possible to see the end of Kerouac's Columbia career as an early instance of his pathological inability to accept discipline in anything bar his own self-imposed writing schedules. The pattern was repeated when he enlisted in – and was soon discharged by – the US Navy: Kerouac clearly had no time for boot camp and one morning he simply laid down his rifle and walked away from drill. To expedite his departure, he was happy both to punch an officer and to feign homosexuality.

Kerouac's next venture was more successful, for reasons that are significant in understanding his career as a writer of novels 'about' his own life. Following his discharge, Kerouac enlisted in the Merchant Marine and sailed for Liverpool on the SS *George Weems*. While crossing the Atlantic at the height of the Second World War was obviously a dangerous business – especially with a cargo of bombs – it was also an opportunity for Kerouac to formulate his dreams about becoming a writer of epic novels in the tradition of Herman Melville and Thomas Wolfe. Ironically, for a man whose fame would later bring an indelible association with the road and the North American continent, this vision originally encompassed the ocean and his own projected epic called 'The Sea Is My Brother'. But, while the locale was to change, the essential components of Kerouac's project were starting to be assembled: the opening paragraph of *On the Road* would echo Ishmael's famous explanation of why he goes to sea at the start of *Moby Dick* and even as early as 1943 Kerouac was imagining a form of fiction that placed his own alter ego confronting social and spiritual alienation and seeking redemption through the philosophical truths revealed by the land/seascape. While it would take Kerouac almost another decade to master his own voice (the 'spontaneous prose' of much of his most famous work), and while his first published novel, *The Town and the City* (1950), would still rely on the structures and rhythms of earlier American writers, Kerouac's months in the Merchant Marine mark the moment when 'The Legend of Duluoz' could be said to have been conceived.

Allen Ginsberg

Kerouac, then, had already experienced life beyond high school and the campus by the time that the seventeen-year-old

Allen Ginsberg arrived at Columbia in 1943. Initially, therefore, although Kerouac (and the older and more experienced William Burroughs) could recognize the sincerity of Ginsberg's vision, they would often treat him as little more than a child, especially since the gawky and bespectacled teenager bore no resemblance to the (by now) former football star. While Ginsberg lacked the physical power and good looks of Kerouac and Cassady, this did not mean that he could not recognize – and fall in love with – these qualities in others. Ginsberg's background is similar to Kerouac's in that he also came from a small industrial town (Paterson, New Jersey), but differs in key respects. First, Ginsberg's parents had acquired considerably more education: his father, Louis, was a schoolteacher and poet and his mother, Naomi, also taught school. In addition, they had political beliefs that would have been anathema to Kerouac's politically and culturally conservative parents – Louis was a socialist and Naomi a communist – and participated in the bohemian life of Greenwich Village around 1920, when they experimented with the then daring free love and trips to nudist camps. Although Naomi suffered the first of a series of nervous breakdowns in 1919, and would be incapacitated by increasingly severe bouts of insanity for the rest of her life, both parents instilled in their sons, Eugene (born in 1921) and Allen, a strong belief in the importance of striving to improve the world.

As a result – and although his initial ambition was to be a labour lawyer defending the oppressed – Ginsberg came from a background within which an ambition to be a creative writer was celebrated rather than being seen as a cause for concern. While Kerouac's journalist-printer father regarded writing as a trade and imagined that his son would utilize his Columbia education to make a fortune as a lawyer or insurance salesman, Ginsberg's father took an active, lifelong interest in his son's poetry. While Louis Ginsberg's own work was based upon a faith in traditional form – a stress on rhyme and conventional structure – this did not mean that he lacked either the interest or the vocabulary to become one of his son's sternest critics, offering the kind of informed, detailed questioning that Kerouac's parents were incapable of providing.

But Ginsberg also brought a darker knowledge with him to Columbia. While Kerouac and Burroughs both flirted with abnormal behaviour – either to call attention to themselves or as a ploy for escaping from undesirable situations – Ginsberg was already familiar with the horrors of the psychotic illness that he had witnessed in his mother during his early teens. While his mother's illness and premature death in 1956 would later result in 'Kaddish' (1961), perhaps his greatest poem, they also left the young man who arrived in New York profoundly concerned about his own sanity. Much of his anxiety revolved around his difficulties (until the 1950s) in accepting his homosexuality; bursts of homosexual activity would be followed by lengthy periods of guilt and depression and – during the early 1950s – by a sustained effort to lead a 'straight' life. But this was not all. Ginsberg also suffered a severe case of what the literary critic Harold Bloom famously labelled the 'anxiety of influence', through which the reading of great poets' work both inspires a writer to write his or her own verse but also fuels a sense of insecurity that this work is derivative and will not endure. Bloom's most significant case studies are the British Romantics seeking to escape the towering presence of John Milton and, ironically, it was the Romantics who cast the longest shadow over Ginsberg. In particular, Ginsberg felt the presence of William Blake, to the extent that in summer 1948 he experienced a sequence of 'visions' in which Blake's voice travelled across time to recite his poems, 'Ah! Sunflower', 'The Sick Rose' and 'The Little Girl Lost'.

Soon after his Blake visions, Ginsberg's crisis deepened and – following his arrest after becoming caught up in the petty

WILLIAM BLAKE

The poet and artist William Blake (1757–1827) is one of the most important influences not only on the American Beat Generation, but also on their English counterparts in the 1960s, such as Michael Horovitz and Tom Raworth. As religious dissenter, political radical and artistic innovator, Blake offered a trifold challenge to dominant cultural forms that provided a clear model for the counterculture of the twentieth century. Additionally, Blake's indomitable determination to continue with his work, despite generally receiving little or no recognition, served for the Beat Generation as a prototype, matched only by Herman Melville, of an artist telling truths simultaneously irrefutable and too awkward for their contemporaries to accept.

As a child, Blake believed that he had experienced a vision of the prophet Ezekiel sitting under a tree and throughout his life he insisted that he saw visions sent by God. Much of Blake's work offers interpretations of these visions in a complementary combination of word and image – a combination that would much later be integral to the multimedia practices of the avant-garde. Blake served an apprenticeship as an engraver and then studied at the Royal Academy, as well as developing an interest in radical politics, especially in support of the American and French Revolutions, which he believed offered previously unimaginable possibilities for human liberty. His politics also extended to opposition to slavery and an impassioned defence of sexual freedom and of women's rights. His unwavering commitment to freedom and challenge to all forms of oppression also explains why Blake became a cult figure for the Beat Generation. The combination of visionary ideology and political and artistic radicalism suggested a figure who had anticipated many of their own beliefs. In this sense, Blake's regular inconsistency of approach becomes a strength for the Beat Generation: like the American Transcendentalists Ralph Waldo Emerson and Walt Whitman, Blake was happy to contradict himself, especially in the dialogues between word and image that occur in his poetry/engraving works. He thus stands as an

WILLIAM BLAKE (*cont.*)

exemplary example of the rejection of the kind of consistent, disciplined individualism championed by advocates of the American Dream.

Blake's belief in the power of the imagination to transcend mere sensory perception has been adopted by many anti-establishment groups and individuals in the past two centuries. It is integral to Transcendental art and, of course, to the Beat belief in the power of a spirit detached from the individual's body. This faith depends on a combination of the rejection of orthodox religion and a faith in individual religious experience – again, a key distinction for many of the Beat Generation, including Allen Ginsberg and Gary Snyder. While it is impossible to list all of his publications here, some of Blake's illustrated books demand special attention for their influence on the Beat Generation and later American counterculture. See, in particular, *Songs of Innocence* (1789), *Songs of Experience* (1794), *America: A Prophecy* (1793), *Visions of the Daughters of Albion* (1793) and *Jerusalem: The Emanation of the Giant Albion* (1804–20).

criminal activities of Herbert Huncke and two of his associates – he checked into the Columbia Presbyterian Psychiatric Institute. This was not the first time that he had received psychiatric care: he had already been compelled to pay regular visits to a psychiatrist after a 1944 incident at Columbia – he had been suspended for a year for allowing Kerouac (who was no longer a welcome presence on campus for the university authorities) to stay in his room and for scrawling 'Fuck the Jews' in the grime that had accumulated on the windowpane, neglected by the room's cleaning woman, whom he suspected of being anti-Semitic. But, despite the circumstances, Ginsberg's first day at the Institute proved propitious: as he sat waiting to be admitted, he was asked, 'Who are you?' by an overweight, bespectacled Jewish inmate who had just returned from a bout of insulin shock treatment. Quoting Dostoyevsky's *The Idiot*, Ginsberg replied, 'I'm Myshkin. Who are you?' The other man – Carl Solomon – responded, 'I'm Krilov,' echoing Ginsberg's allusion with a reference to the nihilistic character from Dostoyevsky's *The Dispossessed*.

Solomon (1928–93) was to become a significant figure in Beat history, although he was not a writer of significance. A prodigiously gifted scholar, he had spent the mid-1940s alternating between terms at the City College of New York and periods at sea and living in France, where he combined an interest in avant-garde art with a lifestyle immersed in a French version of street-level Beat life. Back in New York, he and two friends staged a Dadaist response to a lecture by Wallace Markfield, throwing potato salad at the lecturer in an event recorded by Ginsberg in 'Howl'. Ginsberg seems to have been fascinated by Solomon's life-story and (with much poetic licence) recounts many incidents from it in 'Howl', which is, of course, dedicated to Solomon. But Solomon was not just a source of inspiration for Ginsberg: he was also, as the nephew of A.A. Wyn, who published Ace paperbacks, a vital link to the world of books, and would be influential – during his intermittent bouts of sanity – in the acceptance and publication of William Burroughs's *Junkie*, though also in the rejection of *On the Road*.

William Burroughs

Ginsberg's months of incarceration in 1949 led him to question his relationship with William Seward Burroughs (1914–97), who had been offering him his own form of amateur analysis during the preceding year but was irked by Ginsberg's willingness to accept the advice of his father and his Columbia professors and to seek professional psychiatric help. Burroughs – after Kerouac and Ginsberg, probably the most significant member of the Beat Generation, even if much of his major fiction was only completed and published long after its hip ascendancy had passed – was born in St Louis, Missouri and educated at the Los Alamos Ranch School for boys in New Mexico, where he first realized that he was homosexual, before graduating from Harvard in 1936. He was named after his grandfather, who invented and patented the Burroughs Adding Machine in 1885 and earned a sizeable fortune from its sales. Although Jack Kerouac's claims about Burroughs's inherited wealth were considerably exaggerated (much to the embarrassment and annoyance of Burroughs himself), the legacy from his grandfather's invention did provide a substantial monthly allowance that enabled Burroughs to pursue his interests in the seedier aspects of American life without having to take regular full-time employment. Burroughs was both widely read in literature, philosophy and whatever else caught his interest at a given moment and fascinated with guns, with the workings of petty criminals and with the effects of using different drugs. Already around thirty when he encountered Kerouac, Lucien Carr and Ginsberg, Burroughs was several years older than the other leading Beats and had travelled widely in Europe and the United States before he met them. Famously, he went to study medicine in Vienna and married the Jewish Ilsa Klapper to enable her to escape the Nazis and accompany him to New York. Like most of the other early Beats, Burroughs had a troubled psychiatric history, which he traced back to a half-remembered experience with his governess and her lover when he was a small boy. Soon after his arrival in New York, he sheared off the top of his little finger to demonstrate his love for a male friend and was confined in Bellevue and the Payne–Whitney psychiatric hospitals.

Burroughs had been writing since his early childhood, commencing with a story titled 'The Autobiography of a Wolf' at age eight, which he refused to reclassify as 'Biography' when advised to do so by his parents. His first published essay, 'Personal Magnetism', appeared in 1929 and he continued to write noir thrillers. Despite this, Burroughs didn't really consider himself to be a 'writer' until the 1950s, when Ginsberg and Kerouac encouraged his efforts and attempted to edit his voluminous output into publishable formats. Instead, he flirted unsuccessfully with joining the CIA and, among other short-term jobs, spent several months working as a bug exterminator in Chicago in 1942, an experience that later provided the basis for much of his subsequent writing. Soon after his return to New York, he met with the other Beats and became a kind of mentor to the younger figures.

Burroughs can usefully be placed within a tradition of Anglo-American writers, including Jack London and George Orwell, who put their book knowledge to practical use in the exploration of the lives of the dispossessed and the down and out. In *The People of the Abyss* (1903), London recounts how he disguised himself in a working man's clothes and immersed himself in the squalor of London's East End in an effort to expose the horrors of that world to a genteel readership. In *Down and Out in Paris and London* (1933), Orwell relates a similar – though longer – experience, using autobiographical details to construct a narrative of social deprivation, casual violence and alcoholism. But Burroughs takes the project further: while London kept clean clothes and money in a room nearby and Orwell is often appalled by the demeaning scenes he witnesses, Burroughs is uninterested in making overt social comments from a position outside what he witnesses. For Burroughs, the research involves becoming as much a part of the world he inhabits as is possible and – although he later used incidents from his time on the streets as the basis for long, semi-hallucinogenic scats in novels including *Naked Lunch* and *The Exterminator*, as well as the more realistic *Junkie* – his concern during the 1940s appears to have been more with experience itself than with writing about it.

In New York, Burroughs's time became divided between the world of the nascent Beat Generation and the 'beat' scene of hustling and addiction that existed around Times Square, and that was embodied by Herbert Huncke. This crossover perhaps

HERBERT HUNCKE

Herbert Huncke (1915–96) became the best known of the hustlers, drifters and petty crooks befriended by the Beat Generation around Times Square. Born in Massachusetts and raised by his wealthy family in Chicago, he spent the 1930s combining several stints in prison and freight-hopping treks around the United States. Huncke had settled in Manhattan's Lower East Side by the time he met William Burroughs in 1945, engaging in various criminal escapades and developing a heroin habit. Huncke's diminutive physical presence and sad, lidded eyes gave him a deceptively harmless appearance and – for the Beat Generation – the look of a down-on-his-luck saint. Huncke features in this manner in thinly veiled representations as Herman in Burroughs's first published novel, *Junkie* (1953), and is the model for Junky in Kerouac's *The Town and the City* and Elmo Hassel in *On the Road*.

Although Huncke did publish some stories and poems later in his life, his primary importance to Beat history lies in his impact on major figures rather than in his own writing. He met Burroughs when the latter was attempting to offload a Thompson submachine gun and purchase narcotics, as part of his anthropological effort to experience American subculture. While Huncke initially thought that Burroughs (patently a misfit in this world) was a detective, and so wanted nothing to do with him, his attitude soon changed and he introduced Burroughs to heroin and to the habit that he would feed and break repeatedly throughout the remainder of his life. Huncke's presence would invariably bring trouble for his friends, since he lacked either the energy, the morality or the

HERBERT HUNCKE (*cont.*)

sense of responsibility to protect them from the consequences of his actions. Both Burroughs and Ginsberg were arrested (at different times) as a result of Huncke's proclivity to stash stolen goods in their apartments, but they always seemed willing to forgive him.

If this was all, it would be easy enough to write Huncke off as a junkie hanger-on, preying on the naivety of his literary acquaintances. But Huncke has significance for other reasons: First, he was a gifted storyteller whose ability to create narratives spontaneously – learned during his time as a hobo needing to think on his feet in order to stay fed and out of jail – offered a compositional model to Kerouac that would only later be equalled by Neal Cassady's stream-of-consciousness improvisations about his sexual encounters or his own life on the road as a boy travelling with his alcoholic father. In addition, Huncke introduced Kerouac, Ginsberg and the others to the concept of 'beat', a state in which an individual was 'beaten down' to a point where they had nothing left but subsequently experienced forms of epiphany about the world and individual human existence. Although Huncke did not develop the point himself, it is clear that Kerouac's later extension of 'beat' to include a form of saintly innocence when surrounded by corruption was also modelled upon a highly romanticized view of Huncke.

helps to explain why the largely homosexual Burroughs became attracted to and later married Joan Vollmer (1924–51), another of the founding members of the New York Beat community. Like Burroughs, Vollmer came from a wealthy, upper-middle-class family and was both smart and well educated, having studied at Barnard College, a liberal arts institution for women that has close ties with Columbia University. In Manhattan, she shared an apartment with Edie Parker, later (and briefly) Kerouac's first wife, on 118th Street which rapidly became the meeting place for Kerouac, Burroughs, Ginsberg, Carr and others. By this time, Vollmer had already been married to Paul Adams and given birth to a daughter. Adams, however, had been drafted during the war and did not return until the new Beat group had become established. Adams – a rather straight-laced law student – disapproved of Joan's new friends and of their influence on her and swiftly filed for divorce. Vollmer and Burroughs then commenced an affair instigated by Allen Ginsberg, who felt that the pair's intelligence and interests were ideally matched. This point is debatable: on the one hand, it is clear that the generally homosexual Burroughs felt a strong sexual attraction to Vollmer and by all accounts they experienced a highly active love life and were virtually inseparable; on the other, the relationship led to a swift decline in Vollmer's health and appearance as she embraced the lifestyle embodied by many of Burroughs's hood and hustler acquaintances, developed a serious Benzedrine habit, experienced psychotic episodes and also suffered debilitating after-effects from a bout of polio.

Although Burroughs and Vollmer were never legally married, they did live together as husband and wife and parented William Burroughs, Jr. When Burroughs left New York to live in New Orleans, Vollmer and the children accompanied him in settling in the ramshackle home that is described in *On the Road* (where they are fictionalized as Old Bull Lee and Jane). They subsequently relocated to Mexico City to escape from police interest in Burroughs's drug-related activities. It was here, in 1951, that one of the most notorious incidents in Beat history occurred, when Burroughs shot and killed his wife while attempting to shoot a glass William Tell fashion from the top of her head. Burroughs was charged with murder and detained until his brother arrived and most likely bribed local lawmen to release him, but there has been an ongoing debate ever since over what really happened. For pioneering scholars of Beat such as Ann Charters, the death was a tragic accident, while for others, including Burroughs himself (who was released on bail and fled Mexico after a fortnight's detention), there has been a feeling that the shooting could have been provoked by Burroughs's subconscious urge to free himself from his heterosexual ties. For others, Burroughs's motives were both more straightforward and more sinister: his need to experience all that life could offer included the necessity of discovering what it was like to kill another human being. Whatever actually happened, the incident unsurprisingly haunted Burroughs for the remainder of his life and – as he made clear in the introduction to his novel *Queer*, written two years after Joan's death – was the driving force behind his decision to focus on writing.

Lucien Carr

Joan Vollmer's death is a striking and dramatic moment in Beat history, but it was not the first killing to involve them. While Lucien Carr (1925–2005) was not a Beat writer and spent much of his later life working as an editor for United Press and attempting to distance himself from the notoriety they brought, he was a pivotal figure in introducing the central triumvirate of Burroughs, Ginsberg and Kerouac. Like Burroughs, he grew up in St Louis and came from a wealthy family and, although his father left when Carr was two, his mother was able to send him to private school and to introduce him to foreign travel. Before arriving at Columbia, Carr had studied at the Phillips–Andover Academy in Massachusetts, Bowdoin College and, briefly, at the University of Chicago, during which time he met Burroughs for the first time. In Chicago, Carr attempted suicide by placing his head inside a gas oven, although, characteristically, he claimed that the act was a work of performance art.

Beyond his fundamental role in bringing Ginsberg, Burroughs and Kerouac together, Carr is a significant member of the early Beat Generation for two further reasons: first, he was instrumental in transforming Ginsberg from the idealistic young would-be labour lawyer who arrived in New York into a Rimbaud- and Baudelaire-reading frequenter of Greenwich Village bars. Ginsberg was fascinated both by the gulf between Carr's angelic appearance and his wilfully anti-conventional behaviour (especially when he felt that a situation was becoming dull) and by his language, noting in his diary that to understand Lucien's anarchic presence it was necessary to learn his key words, 'fruit, phallus, clitoris, cacoethes, faeces, foetus, womb, Rimbaud'.

ARTHUR RIMBAUD

Jean Nicolas Arthur Rimbaud (1854–91) was – along with William Blake and Walt Whitman – perhaps the most significant literary influence on Allen Ginsberg and many other Beats. This was as much a result of his lifestyle as of his poetry, most of which was written before his twentieth birthday. Following childhood in Charleville in the Ardennes, where he was an outstanding scholar, Rimbaud ran away from home several times during the chaotic period of the Franco-Prussian War and the Paris Commune in 1871, while also attempting to have his poems published. He was enthusiastically welcomed to Paris by fellow poet Paul Verlaine and rapidly acquired a reputation as an ill-mannered, unkempt, absinthe-drinking troublemaker. Verlaine abandoned his wife to be with Rimbaud and the pair travelled in Belgium and lived in London, where their love affair caused a scandal among the exiled Communards. Following increasingly tempestuous scenes, Verlaine shot Rimbaud in the wrist, as a result of which Verlaine was sentenced to two years' imprisonment for assault. Rimbaud spent the remainder of the 1870s roaming through Europe, usually on foot.

Rimbaud abandoned writing in 1873 and spent periods as a soldier, trader and illegal gun-runner in Abyssinia, dying shortly

ARTHUR RIMBAUD (*cont.*)

after his return to France in 1891. Alongside his verse, he also (in May 1871) wrote the *Lettre du Voyant*, a poetic manifesto that was the inspiration for the proto-Beat 'New Vision' constructed by Carr, Ginsberg and Kerouac in the 1940s. For Rimbaud (as for the Beat Generation), poetry must be the direct product of experience and Vision (*Voyance*) and should replace the reliance on old formal structures with original patterns that transmit the feelings of the poet in as unmediated a manner as possible. The poet must be committed to self-exploration at whatever cost, even if this leads to self-destruction – a commitment that was adopted unreservedly by Kerouac. Rimbaud's advocation of alcohol, drugs, sexual experimentation and solitude served as a model not only for Kerouac's lifelong devotion to his writing, but also anticipated William Burroughs's investigations in its combination of aesthetic experimentation and a desire to understand – and ultimately to change – the social and moral orders.

Rimbaudesque in appearance and behaviour, Carr believed in the deployment of a kind of poetic, performative madness as a means of shaking society free of its rigid norms; he would chew on a beer glass, gnaw on a raw steak or break into obscene song on the subway in efforts to challenge onlookers out of their complacency, a tactic that would later be adapted by Ginsberg himself in actions such as stripping naked during his poetry readings or staring at fellow subway travellers through a hole cut in a newspaper, and by countercultural groups such as Ken Kesey's Merry Pranksters in their travels across the United States.

With Ginsberg, Carr developed the 'New Vision', a loose artistic manifesto that anticipated many key tenets of Beat ideology. For Carr, the term 'New Vision' was 'practically impossible to define . . . It was trying to look at the world in a new light, trying to look at the world in a way that gave it some meaning.

Trying to find values . . . that were valid. And it was through literature that all this was supposed to be done.' For Ginsberg, as noted in his journal at the time, 'Since art is merely and ultimately self-expressive, we conclude that the fullest art, the most individual, uninfluenced, unrepressed, uninhibited expression of art is true expression and the true art.'[2] While such ideas about art were hardly original, with roots in European Romanticism and American Transcendentalism, as well as in the overt influence of Rimbaud on Carr's behaviour, they offer the first, half-formed expression of the Beat Generation's own notions of spontaneity and authenticity as integral to artistic production.

Carr's second principal claim to fame is his role in the first of the two killings that have become immortalized in Beat mythology. At age ten, Carr had met David Kammerer, who was the leader of the Cub Scout pack that Carr attended. Kammerer, who was fourteen years older than Carr, initially acted as a kind of surrogate father, taking Lucien to Mexico and subsequently following him to Andover, Maine, Chicago and, finally, New York. The common belief – accepted by most Beat historians – is that Kammerer was a predatory homosexual, whose unwanted advances confused the young Carr and prompted his suicide attempt. Despite his own background in the higher echelons of Saint Louis, he seemed happy to take whatever menial jobs were available in order to be near Lucien. Oddly, however – if Kammerer is to be viewed as a stalker – Carr did little to discourage the older man's presence and was happy not only to treat him as a friend but also to engage in overtly homoerotic wrestling bouts with him.

In the summer of 1944, Carr decided to try to escape Kammerer's attentions and planned to enlist in the Merchant

---

[2] Both quoted in Barry Miles, *Allen Ginsberg: A Biography* (London: Virgin, 2002), p. 45.

Marine. Kerouac agreed to join him and – with echoes of Rimbaud – they agreed to leave their ship when it reached France and walk to Paris. On 14 August, however, before they had chance to sail, Carr stabbed and killed Kammerer on a bank beside the Hudson River near Riverside Park. According to Carr's own testimony in court, he had been drinking at the West End Bar and, when it closed, the two had gone to sit by the river and continue drinking. Kammerer had made demands for sex and a struggle had ensued, in the course of which Carr had stabbed Kammerer twice with (ironically) his Boy Scout pocket knife. When he realized that Kammerer was dead, he bound his body and weighed it down with stones before rolling it into the river. He then sought out Burroughs, who destroyed an incriminating blood-soaked packet of cigarettes and advised Carr to tell his mother and follow his family's lawyer's instructions. Carr preferred to seek out Kerouac, who helped him to dispose of the knife and Kammerer's spectacles and it was only after the pair had seen a movie and been to the Museum of Modern Art that Carr visited his aunt, who contacted the lawyer.

Once Carr had turned himself in, he was detained without charge – since no body had been found and the Assistant District Attorney was unsure whether the event had actually occurred – and spent his time reading Rimbaud. It was only when the body was located floating in the Hudson that Carr was charged with homicide and Burroughs and Kerouac were arrested as material witnesses, the latter only just avoiding being charged as an accessory to the murder, since he had been with Carr when he disposed of the knife and Kammerer's glasses. Burroughs was quickly freed after his family paid the bail and was swiftly taken to St Louis by his father, but Kerouac's outraged father refused to help and left Kerouac in the Bronx jail. Instead, his girlfriend Edie Parker's mother paid the bail, but only after Kerouac was granted a temporary release from the jail to marry Edie, with two detectives serving as witnesses. Kerouac then also left town, to stay at his new mother-in-law's house in Grosse Point, Michigan.

Carr pleaded guilty to manslaughter and was sentenced to an indeterminate time in prison. He spent two years at Elmira Reformatory, the same time that Verlaine had spent in prison after shooting Rimbaud. He was certainly spared more serious charges and a longer sentence as a result of the defence claims about Kammerer's advances and psychiatric assessments that suggested he could be turned into a 'useful citizen' with the correct treatment.[3] He was also warned that subsequent misbehaviour could result in further detention and, after his release, was keen to distance himself from Beat culture. He requested that his name be removed from the dedications page of *Howl* (where it appeared in the first edition) and made stringent efforts to ensure that he could not be identified from Kerouac's autobiographical fictions, although Kerouac eventually ignored these and told the story in *Vanity of Duluoz* (1968).

Carr's version of events seems to have been accepted not only by the court, but also by the media and, later, by tellers of Beat history such as Barry Miles, James Campbell and Gerald Nicosia. According to the *New York Times*, for example,

> Carr said that he rejected [an offensive proposal from Kammerer] indignantly and that a fight ensued. Carr, a slight youth, 5 feet 9 inches tall and weighing 140 pounds was no match for the burly physical education instructor, who was six feet tall and weighed about 185 pounds. He was rapidly getting the worst of it, he said. In desperation, Carr pulled out of his pocket his boy scout knife . . . and plunged the blade twice in rapid succession into Kammerer's chest.[4]

---

[3] See Barry Miles, *Jack Kerouac, King of the Beats: A Portrait* (London: Virgin, 2002), p. 76.

[4] Quoted in James Campbell, *This Is the Beat Generation: New York, San Francisco, Paris* (London: Secker & Warburg, 1999), pp. 29–30.

It is probably unsurprising that the generally homophobic society of the time was so willing to accept Carr's defence, although it is more curious that it has largely remained unquestioned by scholars. Since Carr's death in 2005, however, doubt has been cast on the official record. Eric Homberger, for example, in a lengthy obituary, points out that:

> Much of the story, however, is doubtful; perhaps now, with Carr's death, it may be possible to disentangle some of the strands of insinuation, legal spin and lies. There is no independent proof that Kammerer was a predatory stalker; there is only Carr's word for the pursuit from St Louis to New York; there is persuasive evidence that Kammerer was not gay. Carr enjoyed his ability to manipulate the older man, and got him to write essays for his classes at Columbia. A friend remembers Kammerer slamming the door of his apartment in Carr's face and telling him to get lost.[5]

The early Beat grouping was relatively short-lived. Carr's detention, Ginsberg's intermittent psychiatric problems, Burroughs's need to lie low, and subsequently to move away from New York with Vollmer, and Kerouac's restlessness all contributed to a disbursing of the community that had created the seeds of the Beat Generation. In any case, Beat history was about to be reshaped by a figure who was vastly different from the college-educated community centred around the Columbia campus.

The road west: Enter Neal Cassady

In the winter of 1946 the dynamics of the New York group were changed for ever by the arrival in New York of Neal

[5] *The Guardian*, 9 February 2005, http://books.guardian.co.uk/obituaries/ story/0,11617,1408971,00.html.

Cassady, the model for *On the Road*'s Dean Moriarty, Hart Kennedy in John Clellon Holmes's *Go* and the 'secret hero' of 'Howl'. Cassady had been born in Salt Lake City in 1926 and had spent his childhood travelling around the western states with his father, a barber whose chronic alcoholism resulted in lengthy periods of unemployment and hoboing. As a result, Cassady had developed a strong sense of independence and – perhaps, less positively – irresponsibility. Despite his showing an aptitude for learning during the periods when he was in one place long enough to attend school regularly, Cassady's youth seems to have been spent largely in Denver pool halls, in stealing cars for kicks and in reform school. In addition, he was also vastly more sexually experienced than Ginsberg and even Kerouac, claiming to have lost his virginity at age nine and to have satiated his immense sexual appetite at every possible opportunity since then. By the time that he arrived in New York, he was married to the teenage LuAnne Henderson, although this did not preclude the constant search for other female companions (most notably, Carolyn Robinson, whom he would marry in 1948) or the affair that he conducted with Allen Ginsberg in the late 1940s.

It is almost impossible to overstate the importance of Cassady to the Beat Generation. In many ways, he can be seen as the magic ingredient that transformed a group of promising but still – in some senses – rather conservative young writers into a movement creating a new art form that would reshape the American culture of the second half of the twentieth century and beyond. And yet, it is hard to regard Cassady himself as a significant writer: his autobiographical account of his childhood, *The First Third* (1971/81), is illuminating in explaining how he became who he was when he arrived in New York, but certainly falls far short of the hyperbolic praise heaped upon it by Kerouac and Ginsberg, who thought that they had discovered a new Proust. Likewise, Cassady's *Collected Letters* (2004) only intermittently capture the energy that the others sensed and that Kerouac claimed shaped his own spontaneous prose. Despite subsequent encouragement from Kerouac and Ginsberg, Cassady always found writing a struggle and even Ginsberg's tireless efforts to champion his works were not enough to make Cassady a literary celebrity, even if he continued to feature as a presence in the literature and music of the 1960s.

Thus, while Cassady's literary outpourings should not be entirely discounted – and the eighteen-thousand-word 'Joan Anderson letter' that he sent Kerouac in December 1950 did indubitably help in refining Kerouac's prose, both in encouraging a more informal style, designed to resemble a letter to a friend, and in persuading Kerouac to highlight the 'kicks' that peppered his travels – it is Cassady's character that is of much greater significance. While many of Ginsberg and Kerouac's more intellectual Columbia friends thought that Cassady was a fool and would have nothing to do with him, Ginsberg and Kerouac understood that his energy and frantic search for kicks offered a vibrant alternative to the ennui and angst that characterized so many of the New York crowd. The figure captured as Dean in *On the Road* is a man seemingly desperate to make up for the time lost in reform school, seeking ecstasy in sex, marijuana, jazz, fast cars and experiencing the American landscape and its peoples. While he is someone intuitively recognized as 'trouble' by institutional figures like the police, elderly relatives and the wives of the friends he encourages to follow him, he offers the chance to share his search with would-be like-minded men desperate to unshackle themselves from the tight chains of post-war American life. As such, he exemplifies the homosocial bonding at the heart of the most famous Beat writing, whether that writing is largely homo- or heterosexual in content.

But that is not all: Cassady was also a mesmeric storyteller, able to hold his audience transfixed for hours at a time while he recounted tales of his early life with his father or of his sexual encounters. While Cassady himself struggled to translate this oral ability into a literary one, Kerouac saw in it the potential to take his own work in a new direction. When Cassady arrived in New York for the first time, Kerouac was working on *The Town and the City*, the book that would be his first published novel. The difference between this – in essence, an effort to write the 'Great American Novel' in the epic tradition of Thomas Wolfe – and what follows is startling and has much to do with Kerouac's ability to hear the rhythms of Cassady's storytelling and transcribe them into written prose. While plainly many other shaping forces underpinned Kerouac's writing – including, for example, jazz, writers of the American Renaissance such as Melville and Whitman and modernist experimenters including Joyce and Faulkner – it was the storytelling ability of Neal Cassady, learned out of necessity during his haphazard and chaotic travels with (and periods of separation from) his father, that enabled Kerouac to translate his own ideas into an idiosyncratic, distinctive style. Cassady seems to have been the inspiration for Kerouac finally making the trips west and to Mexico that would be chronicled in *On the Road*, but – as *On the Road* implies – it was listening to Cassady that gave Kerouac the voice to describe what he was seeing and experiencing.

Other voices: Completing the New York scene

The impact of Neal Cassady on the Columbia crowd was profound and permanent, prompting not only Kerouac's trips to the West Coast, but also Ginsberg's brief move to Denver and contributing to his later decision to move to the Bay region. He was not, however, the last of the significant early Beats to join the East Coast crowd. Both John Clellon Holmes (1926–88) and

Gregory Corso (1930–2001) would also have a profound influence on the birth and development of Beat and both would play important roles at key moments of Beat history. Ironically, given the pre-eminence of Kerouac, Ginsberg and Burroughs within the Beat Generation, both would also publish significant – and successful – books before the appearance of 'Howl' and *On the Road*.

Like Kerouac, Holmes came from Massachusetts, although his upbringing in Holyoke was considerably more genteel. After spending the final two years of the war serving in the Hospital Corps of the US Navy, he enrolled at Columbia to study literature and philosophy. Unlike the members of the group that had met around the Columbia campus in the preceding years, Holmes was living a relatively stable life as a married man and nascent New York intellectual. Nevertheless, he was already feeling a sense of alienation and willingness to embrace both the existential philosophy that was reaching across the Atlantic from France and the Bebop jazz that promised liberation from the square world of his bookish friends. On 4 July 1948, he tagged along with Alan Harrington, a friend of Allen Ginsberg, to Ginsberg's Independence Day party in the Spanish Harlem apartment where he had recently experienced his Blake visions. Holmes was a naturally retiring man – sometimes labelled the 'Quiet Beat' – and withdrew from the frenetic combination of shouting and music to look at the fine collections of first-edition eighteenth-century verse and religious textbooks belonging to Ginsberg's landlord, the theology student Russell Durgin, and later stolen and sold by Herbert Huncke. Kerouac had also withdrawn from the party and the two rapidly struck up a conversation that would lead to a friendship that would last for the rest of Kerouac's life.

Holmes was an intellectual and an observer, astute in his abilities to recognize and record what was significant about Kerouac, Ginsberg and others, but either incapable of or unwilling to indulge in their more extreme patterns of behaviour. He was fascinated by the combination of creativity and intelligence that they applied to their attacks on the norms of respectable, white America and quickly became a student and chronicler of Beat life. Kerouac lent him the manuscript of *The Town and the City* within weeks of their first meeting and Holmes also persuaded Ginsberg to hand over his poems and notebooks, which proved invaluable in providing the details that Holmes would recite in *Go*, his debut novel, published in 1952. There were, however, limits to Holmes's embrace of the emergent Beat scene and his inescapably square persona was incapable of understanding the appeal Neal Cassady held for Kerouac and Ginsberg.

Beat mythology suggests that Kerouac and Holmes invented the term 'Beat Generation', Holmes recognizing the significance of a passing comment that Kerouac made in trying to sum up the group's place in American life. But while Kerouac is unquestionably recognized as 'King of the Beats', the lengthy period of revisions and rejections between the first draft of *On the Road* and its publication meant that the phrase 'Beat Generation' first appeared in Holmes's *Go*. To see the patiently researched and revised *Go* as a novel bearing any more than a passing resemblance to Kerouac's fiction – or to the key tenets of Kerouac and Ginsberg's compositional and ideological emphasis on spontaneity – would be misleading. Where *On the Road*'s Sal Paradise is very much a part of the underground community that this character describes – even if he does make regular trips home to his aunt's and spends much of the novel observing Dean – Paul Hobbes, the protagonist of *Go*, is on the margins of that world. As a self-styled alienated intellectual, living in a depressingly dark apartment and trapped in a marriage that gives little satisfaction either to himself or to his wife, Kathryn, Hobbes is fascinated by the antics of a group of acquaintances that includes fictional representations of Kerouac (Gene Pasternak) and Ginsberg (David Stofsky). Nevertheless, Hobbes is too much of a square to behave like they do, and feels that they

lacked any caution . . . They made none of the moral or political judgements that he thought essential; they did not seem
compelled to fit everything into the pigeon holes of a system
. . . they seemed to have an almost calculated contempt for
logical argument. They operated on feelings, sudden reactions,
expanding these far out of perspective to see in them profundi-
ties which Hobbes was certain they could not define if put
to it.[6]

Where Pasternak acts upon his dream of travelling around
the United States, Hobbes lies about a plan to go to Mexico;
while he professes the desire for an open marriage, he finds it
hard to accept Kathryn's relationship with Pasternak, and (in a
moment symbolic of his more general impotence) loses his
erection just before he can consummate his relationship with
another woman. Thus, while Hobbes's comments about
Pasternak and Stofsky do offer a valid critique of some aspects of
Beat behaviour, and while Holmes constructs an ironic gap
between Hobbes and a more knowing narrator, *Go* does not
offer a representation of the early Beat community from the
inside.

While Kerouac was generally supportive of his friends' efforts
to publish their work, and regarded Holmes as a friend, he was
also envious of the success of a writer whom he regarded as
usurping his rightful position as chronicler of the changes starting to affect American youth. Moreover, as a man always aware
of the significance of money (and his lack of it), he was upset to
learn that Holmes had received a US$20,000 advance for *Go*,
while he had received US$1000 for *The Town and the City* and
was struggling to place a stack of manuscripts that was growing
at the rate of around two books per year in the first half of the

[6] John Clellon Holmes, *Go* (New York: Thunder's Mouth Press, 1988),
p. 35.

1950s. Even if Kerouac's own belief that he was the greatest living writer in America rarely wavered, he still sought critical and commercial recognition to confirm the point. Once more, his relatively humble small-town roots and second-generation immigrant's respect for the views of the American cultural elite meant that he craved their acceptance. Yet, while Holmes's novel was drawing attention to the Beat Generation in a manner that outstripped the occasional extracts that Kerouac *did* manage to publish, his own success tended to feel as far away as ever.

Allen Ginsberg's brief spell in jail and longer time in the Psychiatric Institute seem to have quelled – at least, temporarily – his appetite for 'deviant' behaviour. Like Lucien Carr, who was dedicating himself to life as a journalist with the United Press, Ginsberg began a period of several years in which he would work in marketing and live largely as a heterosexual, with a series of significant girlfriends. To an outsider, it would probably appear that his psychiatric treatment had been a success, in the sense (accepted at the time) that analysis and other forms of treatment were designed to 'normalize' an individual whose internal mechanisms had become 'broken'. This did not mean, however, that Ginsberg entirely abandoned his old haunts and in mid-1950 he called in for a drink at the Pony Stable, a lesbian bar on 3rd Street, where he struck up a conversation with a handsome young Italian American named Gregory Corso. Whereas John Clellon Holmes was a quiet observer and college-educated intellectual, Corso was an outgoing street punk who, like Cassady, had spent time in juvenile detention centres and lived rough on the streets. Born in Little Italy, Corso had no recollection of his mother and had lived with several sets of step-parents during his early childhood. When America entered the Second World War, his father arrived to claim him in the mistaken belief that being the sole carer for a child would make him exempt from the draft and – when Corso, Sr was conscripted into the navy – Gregory was left to fend for himself on the streets of New York.

Corso's teens were spent committing petty crimes in a struggle to survive and in adult prisons, Bellevue Psychiatric Hospital and juvenile detention centres. As a result, he was precociously streetwise and deeply traumatized by age fifteen and embarked on a brief career in armed robbery that resulted in a three-year stretch in Clinton Prison in upper New York State which had ended shortly before he met Ginsberg. This narrative could have developed into one that mirrored the crime–jail cycle experienced by people like Herbert Huncke, but Corso was smart enough to spend his time in prison in a thorough process of self-education, facilitated by the extensive library left in the prison by Mafia boss Charles 'Lucky' Luciano. Since he had no guidance on where to start, he commenced with the birth of European artistic and philosophical life in ancient Greece and Rome and acquired the knowledge of classical culture that would later infuse his own poetry. By the time that he met Ginsberg, Corso already considered himself to be a poet and habitually carried his work under his arm, ready to read to an interested new acquaintance or to be delivered impromptu to an unsuspecting crowd.

While Corso was both the youngest of the central figures of the early New York Beat scene and the last to join their circle, he was also among the first to be published and to receive critical acclaim. His well-received first collection, *The Vestal Lady on Brattle and Other Poems* (1955) was part-funded by Harvard students and appeared before *Howl* and *On the Road* and, although Kerouac and Burroughs had already published other novels by this time, their work had made relatively little impression. Corso's verse from later in the 1950s consolidated his reputation: the publication of *Gasoline* (1958) by San Francisco's City Lights cemented his position as a major Beat writer and while the broadside 'Bomb' (1958) caused controversy among the generally anti-war poetry community with its structural and thematic embrace of the beauty of an atomic explosion, Corso's status as a writer was undiminished.

By the early 1950s, New York's position at the heart of Beat life was under threat. Kerouac had been crossing and recrossing the continent either with Cassady or in pursuit of him since 1947; Ginsberg had spent time in Denver and elsewhere and then moved to San Francisco, where Cassady had already settled; and Burroughs was long gone, living in Texas, New Orleans and Mexico and travelling in South America. The 'hot' environment of Greenwich Village in the 1940s was being replaced by a new 'cool' scene, depicted by Kerouac in *The Subterraneans* (although he makes an unconvincing gesture at disguising the new world by relocating it to San Francisco) and the cool crowd were open in their sneering hostility to Kerouac and his search for kicks. The next phase of Beat activity, which would culminate with the appearance of *Howl* in 1956, took place across the continent in San Francisco, where another community of young, like-minded writers was already assembling and would embrace the migrants from New York.

3

Beat and the San Francisco renaissance

The death of Joan Vollmer can be seen as marking the end of the first period of the Beat Generation's existence. In late summer 1951, Allen Ginsberg and Lucien Carr stayed with Vollmer in Mexico City (William Burroughs was away with a boyfriend) while attending the wedding of one of Carr's work colleagues. Vollmer bore little physical resemblance to the young woman they had known in New York. As a result of polio, she walked with a limp; her teeth had rotted owing to her Benzedrine habit and she was drinking heavily. The trip was marked by Carr's drunken behaviour and by a feeling in Ginsberg's mind that the twenty-seven-year-old Joan was resigned to death. A few days after his return to the United States, he read a newspaper headline reporting that an American tourist had killed his wife while attempting to shoot a glass off her head. The first phase of Beat history was thus book-ended by the killings of David Kammerer by Lucien Carr and Joan Vollmer by William Burroughs.

Ginsberg lived in New York for another two years, continuing his analysis, working as an independent market researcher and striving to remain heterosexual. Despite a few gay encounters, his principal relationships were with women and he even proposed marriage to one – Dusty Moreland – although she rejected the offer. It was during this period that the free verse style, with the rhythm of lines determined by breath-stops and the time it took to express any given image, took shape, under the influence not just of Kerouac and the sounds and rhythms of jazz but also of William Carlos Williams, who was both an internationally renowned exponent of 'American' verse and a resident of Ginsberg's hometown, Paterson, New Jersey. This

WILLIAM CARLOS WILLIAMS

William Carlos Williams (1883–1963) was the most significant influence on Allen Ginsberg in the years leading to the publication of *Howl and Other Poems*. Following Ginsberg's departure from Columbia, Williams succeeded the Columbia professor and cultural critic Lionel Trilling (1905–75) as a kind of spiritual father and mentor to Ginsberg, directly and indirectly encouraging him to reject formal verse and listen to the rhythms of American speech.

Born in Rutherford, New Jersey, a suburb of Paterson, Williams was a near neighbour of the Ginsbergs. Following schooling in Geneva and Paris, he had attended Horace Mann School – where Kerouac would later spend a year in preparation for Columbia – before studying medicine at the University of Pennsylvania. During his years in Philadelphia, Williams met Ezra Pound and Hilda Doolittle and began the pattern of combining writing poetry and practising medicine that would continue until his retirement from medical practice in the early 1950s. During his internship in New York, Williams mixed with the bohemian artistic community and published his first volume of verse, before marrying and returning to Paterson to establish his medical career.

Although Williams did visit Europe again in the 1920s, he differed from the Lost Generation writers in his refusal to abandon the United States and in his insistence that America provided appropriate subject matter for an artist. Thus, while he was friends with Man Ray and Marcel Duchamp, and was heavily influenced by Dadaism (at least, in his early work), he was opposed to the manner in which Pound and T.S. Eliot drew upon classical allusions and languages in their verse. Instead, Williams encouraged poets

WILLIAM CARLOS WILLIAMS (*cont.*)

to use their eyes and ears, reporting what they saw around them in the language of their own neighbourhood. In his own work, this approach is best captured in his prose/poetry epic, *Paterson* (published in five volumes, between 1946 and 1958), and it was only towards the end of his life that his oeuvre was widely recognized as matching the importance of Eliot and Pound's verse.

Williams acknowledged that Ginsberg had provided some of the inspiration for the concluding section of *Paterson*, but Williams's influence on the Beat Generation is much more profound. He was a friend and mentor to Charles Olsen and Kenneth Rexroth, while Gary Snyder suggests that a lecture delivered by Williams at Reed College, when he, Philip Whalen and Lew Welch were students and room-mates there, was instrumental in their own decisions to become poets. Ginsberg sent Williams a long letter and nine of his poems in 1950 after hearing him read in New York, but Williams seems to have been more impressed with the letter – which he included in *Paterson* – than the verse, which was too symbolic for a writer who most famously summed up his own philosophy in the line, 'No ideas but in things.' Ginsberg would subsequently adopt this approach himself, and it is at the core of his most famous poems. Williams wrote an introduction for *Howl and Other Poems*, famously concluding, 'Hold back the edges of your gowns, Ladies, we are going through hell,' but, although he clearly recognized the horrors that Ginsberg had suffered before he could write such verse, he remained ambivalent about Beat poetry, which he felt lacked the disciplined form inherent to all great art.

was the form that Ginsberg would subsequently use for 'Howl' and for many of his other major poems, and Williams would later write the introduction to the City Lights collection of Ginsberg's *Howl and Other Poems*.

Ginsberg was, however, just about the only one of the original gang to remain in New York. With Joan dead, Burroughs travelled in South America, looking for yagé, a consciousness-expanding plant generally used by shamans during religious rituals and – as Burroughs discovered – including severe vomiting among its side effects. Although Burroughs did return briefly to New York, and started to shape the ideas that would eventually be published as *Naked Lunch*, Ginsberg was unwilling to accept his sexual advances and proclamations of love, and Burroughs moved first to Europe and then to Tangier, not returning to the United Sates on a permanent basis for the next two decades. Kerouac was hiding from his estranged second wife, Joan Haverty, in a bid to avoid maintenance payments towards the support of his daughter, Jan (1952–96), and was living with the Cassadys and in fleapit hotels while working on the railroad in California and experiencing his most creative phase as a writer. Corso also moved, briefly, to San Francisco in 1952 and although Carr was around and prone to sporadic revivals of his old habits, he was recently married as well as busy developing his career with the United Press. Huncke was still in jail as a result of the stolen property bust that had briefly implicated Ginsberg, and the latter's relationship with John Clellon Holmes was frosty owing to Holmes's representation of Ginsberg (and, in particular, of his Blake visions) in *Go*.

Unsurprisingly, Ginsberg felt that he needed to escape from New York City, where he had spent most of the previous decade and – following several months exploring Mayan ruins in Mexico – arrived at the Cassadys' house in San Jose, California just too late to meet Kerouac, who had returned to the east to see his mother ('Mémère'). The stay with the Cassadys was short-lived and uncomfortable, and ended abruptly when Carolyn walked in on Cassady and Ginsberg in bed together and ordered the latter from the house – although she did drive him to Berkeley. Living in San Francisco, and again employed in market relations, Ginsberg began a new relationship with a twenty-two-year-old blonde woman named Sheila Williams

Boucher, which he alternated (and, at least once, combined) with sexual liaisons with Cassady whenever the latter's railroad work took him into the city.

Despite bouts of self-loathing, Ginsberg seems to have been reasonably content in his 'respectable' new life involving a steady girlfriend, well-paid job and spacious apartment, but the arrangement was short-lived. He swiftly established contacts with local poets Robert Duncan and Jack Spicer and with Kenneth Rexroth, another writer, two decades older than Ginsberg and regarded as something of a father figure to the alternative San Francisco poetry scene, later to be labelled the 'San Francisco Renaissance'.

KENNETH REXROTH

Although Kenneth Rexroth (1905–82) would become a bitter enemy of Jack Kerouac, and the pair would trade insults via Kerouac's unflattering representation of 'Rheinhold Cacoethes' in *The Dharma Bums* and Rexroth's savage reviews of *On the Road* and *The Subterraneans* in the *San Francisco Chronicle*, Rexroth's influence on the West Coast Beat scene and the San Francisco Renaissance was immense. Born in South Bend, Indiana, Rexroth was an orphan by the age of thirteen and lived with his aunt in Chicago, before hitchhiking around the country in his teens, spending a short time in jail, contemplating becoming a monk, travelling in Mexico, visiting Paris and, finally, moving to San Francisco in 1927. Largely autodidactic, Rexroth had an immense knowledge of literatures from many countries, and translated work into English from Greek, French, Chinese and Japanese originals. His range of interests included Eastern religion, Transcendentalism (especially the life and works of Henry David Thoreau), anarchist politics, painting and French poetry, but he also had wide experience of manual labour, having worked as a docker, fire lookout, farmhand and hospital attendant. Although his own verse went through

KENNETH REXROTH (*cont.*)

many different phases, he was – in all but name – a 'Beat' decades before the Beat Generation emerged, hitchhiking, performing his poetry to jazz accompaniment and celebrating the traditions and freedoms associated with the West. Gary Snyder, in particular, can be seen to have inherited many of Rexroth's ideals in his combination of ecological fervour, mountain climbing, anarchist politics and dedication to Eastern poetry and philosophy.

It is unsurprising that Allen Ginsberg sought out Rexroth soon after he moved to California. The older poet was the hub of the vibrant San Francisco poetry community and held regular 'seminars' at his house, where poets such as Robert Duncan, Phil Lamantia and Jack Spicer would mix with local anarchists, read new work and discuss art and politics. Although much of Rexroth's own poetry now sounds dated, it was a significant factor in Ginsberg's development: many of the themes from Rexroth's 'Thou Shalt Not Kill' (1953), written upon hearing of the death of Dylan Thomas and centred around the castigation of an American society that he blamed for destroying the talents and ambitions of the country's young men, resurface (in very different form) in 'Howl'.

Rexroth had long dreamed of San Francisco starting a revolution in American poetry, but it seems that the emergence of the Beat Generation and the San Francisco Renaissance represented something of a pyrrhic victory for him. In addition to his spats with Kerouac, he was critical of Corso, Ginsberg and (astutely) of the commercialization of Beat culture and the emergence of the beatnik, in a process whereby 'dissent has become a hot commodity'. Much of Rexroth's disquiet stemmed from his disapproval of the behaviour of leading Beats – Kerouac getting drunk and becoming obnoxious, Ginsberg stripping naked during performances, Corso not paying sufficient attention to his appearance – but his attitude was also (unsurprisingly) shaped by the collapse of his marriage after his wife conducted an affair with Ginsberg's friend, the Black Mountain poet Robert Creeley.

But perhaps the most significant event in the transformation of Ginsberg into the Beat and countercultural icon of popular memory is traceable to his first meeting with Peter Orlovsky (b. 1933), a Russian American from Northport, Long Island. Ginsberg had become friendly with Robert LaVigne, a talented young artist, and was struck by a painting of a naked male that was displayed on the wall of LaVigne's North Beach apartment. When he inquired about the model, LaVigne called Orlovsky through from the adjoining room and introduced them. Although they would have periods of separation, and despite the fact that Orlovsky's inclinations were primarily heterosexual, the two would be together for much of the remainder of Ginsberg's life, in a relationship that confirmed to Ginsberg not only his homosexuality but also the need to stay true to his own inclinations and beliefs.

The San Francisco poetry scene

The community of writers that Ginsberg encountered and joined when he moved to San Francisco was a vital element in the revolution in American poetry that occurred in the 1950s. The poets emerging from the Bay area and the New York Beats who joined them on the West Coast can be placed alongside figures associated with the experimental liberal arts institution Black Mountain College, North Carolina (including Charles Olson, Robert Creeley, Robert Duncan, Ed Dorn and Denise Levertov) and the Confessional Poets (most notably, Robert Lowell, Sylvia Plath, John Berryman and Theodore Roethke) in articulating a shared rejection of the traditional (in structure, detached and ironic tone, and restrained voice) verse that was taught and written about by academic critics. There is much overlap between the different groups – and Black Mountain poets such as Creeley and Duncan feature heavily in the San Francisco Renaissance –

and all express deeply personal feelings of frustration, alienation and often despair at the stifling conformity of American life at mid-century and at the refusal of the poetry 'establishment' to look outside New Critical approaches and the veneration of T.S. Eliot. By the mid-1950s, such links were instrumental in transforming the Beat Generation from the small isolated group of New York based writers that I have discussed in the previous chapter into an integral component of an artistic avant-garde with bases not only in New York and San Francisco but also in other major American cities such as Boston and Chicago.

By this time, Kerouac was involved in a detailed study of Buddhism and – with Ginsberg following leads provided by Rexroth – it was inevitable that the easterners would seek out a Berkeley based young poet with western credentials to match Neal Cassady's. Gary Snyder (b. 1930) had grown up in the logging regions of Oregon and Washington State and provided as much of a counterpoint to the cynical New York intellectuals whom Kerouac despised as had the young Cassady almost a decade before. A small, wiry, jeans-wearing devotee of the Wobblies and of ancient Japanese and Chinese poetry and philosophy, Snyder was a serious scholar of Buddhism and of Native American cultures, who was preparing to move to Japan and whose modern-day take on Thoreauvian self-sufficiency made him an obvious hero-in-waiting for Kerouac. Snyder's primary concern was – and has remained – the environment, and he spent his summers working as a fire lookout in the Gifford Pinchot National Forest in Washington State until, bizarrely, he was dismissed because his leftist leanings were considered to be a security risk. Although his neat, Eastern-influenced verse bore little or no resemblance to the material that Ginsberg and Kerouac were now composing, Snyder's combination of practical skills, interest in sexual experimentation and commitment to poetry and learning made him a natural ally to the Beat Generation.

Many of the writers that Ginsberg and Kerouac discovered in San Francisco had shared origins that bore striking parallels to their own early gatherings around Columbia. For example, they struck up friendships with Phil Whalen (1923–2002) and Lew Welch (1926–71), both of whom had roomed with Snyder at Reed College in Portland, Oregon. Whalen had roots similar to Snyder's and had laboured in shipyards and factories, as well as working on the assembly line building B-17 planes during the war and serving as a fire lookout. A devotee of Ezra Pound, he was as interested as Snyder in Eastern poetry and philosophy (later becoming a Zen priest), and shared Snyder's interest in developing verse based on Chinese and – more importantly, for Whalen – Japanese models, but resonating with American themes. Welch was also very much a backwoodsman by incli-nation, as well as being a talented poet and heavy drinker – a pairing that would make him an attractive companion for Kerouac. Like many of the New York Beats, he had suffered a mental breakdown and had failed to complete his graduate studies, and he was working as a taxi driver in San Francisco. Welch was renowned for his driving skills – which were admired to an extent that roused some envy in Cassady – and later drove Kerouac back across the continent while the pair composed poems published as *Trip Trap* (1973). By that time, Welch had been missing for two years, presumed dead after walking into the mountains above Snyder's house north of Nevada City, California with a rifle.

The Six Gallery reading

One of the best known passages from *The Dharma Bums* is Jack Kerouac's reconstruction of the famous 13 October 1955 poetry reading at San Francisco's Six Gallery, where Allen Ginsberg read 'Howl' for the first time and fellow poets Snyder, Whalen,

Michael McClure and Philip Lamantia also performed. Ginsberg, Snyder and Rexroth had planned the event as a means of promoting the local poetry scene and Ginsberg composed a short announcement naming the poets who would read and the date, which was distributed on postcards in the region to advertise the evening. The card concluded,

> Six poets at the Six Gallery. Kenneth Rexroth, M.C. Remarkable collection of angels, all gathered at once in the same spot. Wine, music, dancing girls, serious poetry, free satori. Small collection for wine and postcards. Charming event.[1]

In his biography of Ginsberg, Barry Miles has succinctly summarized the scene that evening:

> The Six Gallery was a converted auto-repair shop at Union and Fillmore. At one end was a small stage, on which [were] arranged six large chairs in a semicircle. Jack and Allen arrived with Lawrence Ferlinghetti and his wife, Kirby, to find over a hundred people squeezed into the small space. The whole bohemian poetry intelligentsia of the Bay area appeared to be gathered together in one room for the first time, and there was an atmosphere of great gaiety and excitement. For most of the poets, including Allen, it was their first public reading.[2]

In retrospect, the night can be seen as the moment that initiated the Beat Generation's transformation from a small underground network of writers to an internationally recognizable 'Generation'. Rexroth, dressed in bow tie and coat, introduced the speakers, moving to the front of the stage each time to utter

---

[1] Quoted in Barry Miles, *Allen Ginsberg: A Biography* (London: Virgin, 2000), p. 192.
[2] Ibid.

a few witticisms and prepare the audience for what would follow. San Francisco local Philip Lamantia (1927–2005), who had been publishing his work in major poetry magazines since the age of fifteen, was the first of the group to perform, although instead of reciting his own work he elected to read selections from the poetry of John Hoffman – an acquaintance of Carl Solomon – who had recently died in Mexico City. Next came Michael McClure (b. 1932), a handsome twenty-two-year-old who would go on to become one of the leading writers of the 1960s countercultural scene. McClure (born on Rimbaud's birthday, 20 October) grew up in Kansas and Washington State and, like many of the West Coast Beats, combined his interests in poetry with a love of nature and the study of anthropology. He arrived in San Francisco in 1954 with ambitions to be a painter in the Abstract Expressionist style of Mark Rothko and Clyfford Still, but enrolled in a poetry workshop conducted by Robert Duncan at San Francisco State College. Duncan urged McClure to be more experimental and to break free from the conventional forms he deployed in his verse, but it was only after meeting Ginsberg that McClure started to gain the confidence to develop his own style. In another of the striking coincidences that attracted members of the Beat Generation to one another, McClure and Ginsberg quickly discovered that they had both experienced Blake visions, Blake having appeared in one of McClure's teenage dreams. At the Six Gallery gathering, where he met Snyder and Whalen for the first time, McClure read 'Point Lobos: Animism' and 'For the Death of 100 Whales', an outraged response to an April 1954 *Time* magazine feature on how GIs in the Antarctic had alleviated their boredom by using their rifles and machine guns to kill a pack of killer whales. The poem not only illustrates McClure's (lifelong) commitment to environmentalism; it also marks a transitional moment in his verse, since he composed it in traditional ballad form but then cut and reassembled the words to make what he called a Cubist poem. The first half of the evening's entertainment was brought to a close by Whalen, who read what Ginsberg described as 'a series of very personal relaxed, learned mystical-anarchist poems . . . written in post-Poundian assemblages of blocks of hard images set in juxtapositions, like haikus'.

After the break, Ginsberg moved to the front of the stage to read the first two sections of 'Howl'. McClure recalls that it was 'like a hot bop scene. Ginsberg was real drunk and he swayed back and forth. You could feel the momentum building up and some of the people began to shout "Go! Go!"'[3] Similarly, in Kerouac's reconstruction in *The Dharma Bums*, Alvah Goldbook's (Ginsberg's) rendition of 'Wail' ('Howl') resembles a 'hot jam session' and stands apart from the works of the other poets, who are all either native westerners or else long-time residents on the West Coast. It was left to Gary Snyder to attempt to follow the rapturous response to 'Howl', which he did with readings from *Myths and Texts*, an epic poem that he had been composing for several years.

Everyone in the audience appears to have sensed that Ginsberg's words – and the manner in which they were delivered – represented a break with the past and signified the start of a new era in poetry and counterculture. For Rexroth, the evening marked the culmination of years of work championing the West Coast poetry scene and the emergence of the San Francisco Renaissance, an artistic breakthrough whose setting – the most liberal of American cities and one largely untainted by a history of puritanical Protestantism – was particularly apt for a movement celebrating the combination of free verse and free love. After the reading, the poets and their friends extended their evening, first by going for a Chinese meal, then by heading to the Place, an artists' bar on Grant Street and finally by having an orgy.

---

[3] Both quoted in James Campbell: *This Is the Beat Generation: New York, San Francisco, Paris* (London: Secker & Warburg, 1999), pp. 180–81.

WALT WHITMAN

Place a copy of 'Howl' alongside sections of 'Song of Myself', Walt Whitman's celebration of the United States as an independent nation, and the physical resemblance is unmistakable. The poems share a free verse form in which each line captures a single image, with continuity maintained through repetition of a key word or phrase at the start of each line (rather than through rhyme or rhythm located at the end). Although Whitman's poem is considerably more upbeat about the state of America than Ginsberg's, the writers share an understanding of the symbiotic relationship between self and nation and draw upon numerous examples to illustrate the point.

Whitman (1819–92) was the second of nine children and was raised in Brooklyn, where he received a rudimentary formal education, but – through his father – became well versed in the abolitionist and utopian ideals of Robert Dale Owen and Fanny Wright. He started work at age eleven and spent the next twenty-five years working as printer, journalist, schoolteacher and publisher. Although he did write some poetry during this period, it was mostly filler material for newspapers and bore no real resemblance to what would follow. In 1855, in his mid-thirties, Whitman issued the first edition of *Leaves of Grass*, a collection striking for its rejection of the formal epic style that dominated nineteenth-century American verse. There is still considerable mystery about how Whitman conceived and developed such a radical book, given that he published nothing to resemble it beforehand and offered no clues about its gestation in *Specimen Days* (1881), an autobiography that is remarkably evasive about much of his life before the Civil War. The first edition of *Leaves of Grass* completely reimagined the role of the poet in American society: instead of the poet's name, the frontispiece was a daguerreotype reproduction of an illustration of Whitman clad in a working man's clothes and clearly dressed for the outdoors – a combination that marked Whitman's interest in the new and the everyday and his status as a man of the people, all of which contrasted with the standard image of 'the poet' at the time. A lengthy preface revealed

WALT WHITMAN (*cont.*)

Whitman's strong commitment to Transcendentalism – and especially to the work of Ralph Waldo Emerson – and outlined his vision of an America where poets, rather than presidents, would lead a utopian community. In one key aspect, Whitman differed from Emerson, Thoreau and other Transcendentalists. In the opening poem (untitled in 1855, but later named 'Song of Myself'), Whitman claimed to be the poet of the body as well as the soul, and his verse is laden with representations of homosexual and heterosexual intimacy. The ease and freedom with which Whitman discussed sex were integral to his identification by Ginsberg and many other Beats as their spiritual forebear.

Whitman always considered *Leaves of Grass* to be a work-in-progress, rather than a finished text. Because he imagined it as a commentary on the state of America, he constantly revised poems and added new ones in a series of reissues that continued until his death. His sense that the poet and his work compose an organic whole and that one must reflect the other is also something inherited by the Beat Generation – think, for example, of Kerouac's 'Legend of Duluoz'. By the end of his life, Whitman was recognized as a major poet. The process had, however, taken several decades. Emerson enthusiastically greeted the first edition of *Leaves of Grass*, but backtracked when he realized the extent of its sexual imagery and was offended when Whitman – a committed self-promoter who was also happy to write and publish his own rhapsodic reviews of *Leaves of Grass* – published a private letter from Emerson praising the book. Like Ginsberg three-quarters of a century later, Whitman fell foul of the censors when the Boston District Attorney and the New England Society for the Suppression of Vice sought the withdrawal and destruction of the 1882 edition, which they deemed obscene. Although Whitman was willing to make some changes to his text, he would not compromise on the demand that some poems should be removed and agreed, instead, to have his work published in Philadelphia. As would later be the case with 'Howl', the publicity did Whitman no harm, raising both book sales and national awareness of the poet.

Kerouac and Ginsberg were both, of course, easterners, and 'Howl', with its Whitmanesque structure and resemblances to Kerouac's *The Subterraneans* (see chapter 4), remains very much a product of New York. The poem is urban and – like Kerouac's best prose and verse – can best be appreciated when read aloud. In contrast, the other poets at the Six Gallery are often more concerned with rural scenes – or at least with incidents that represent significant philosophical and geographical distance from New York and East Coast ideologies – and observe the decline of America from the far side of an ever-diminishing pre-industrial frontier, perhaps existing solely in their imaginations. While all of these poets became significant figures in Beat literature, it was Ginsberg and 'Howl' that made the deepest and most long-lasting impression. In its published form, the poem opens with probably the best-known counter-cultural assault on the stultifying destruction of the individual by authoritarian surveillance and control: Ginsberg sees the 'best minds of my generation destroyed by madness, starving, hysterical naked, / dragging themselves through the Negro streets at dawn looking for an angry fix',[4] in a lengthy confessional account of his own and his friends' mental instability and turn to drugs, jazz, alcohol and (homosexual) sex as alternatives to the oppressive worlds of the university and the workplace which had been unavoidable during his years in New York. Following the highly personal narratives of section 1, part 2 of 'Howl' constitutes a direct and sustained attack on a commodity-obsessed society willing to sacrifice its children to an obsession with profit. Using imagery reminiscent of the closing chapters of Herman Melville's *Pierre* (1852), Ginsberg berates a culture so beholden to wealth that it is blind to beauty and condemns emotion. This society – named 'Moloch' in the poem after the

---

[4] Allen Ginsberg, 'Howl', in *Howl and Other Poems* (San Francisco: City Lights, 1956), p. 9.

Canaanite fire god for whom parents burned their children in sacrifice – is seen as a machine, a prison, a 'cannibal dynamo' and the home of 'granite cocks! monstrous bombs!' and Ginsberg expresses anxiety about the difficulties inherent to avoiding complicity with its systems. Therefore, the final section, with its repeated refrain, 'I'm with you in Rockland,' also appears to look back to the Transcendentalists, in this case to find a space from which to critique society. In 'Resistance to Civil Government' (1849), Thoreau suggested that, 'Under a government which imprisons any unjustly, the true place for a just man is also a prison.'[5] In an age where analysis was often seen as little more than the chance to retune 'malfunctioning' individuals (such as homosexuals) and adjust them in anticipation of a return to 'normal' life, for Ginsberg – as later for the Beat-influenced Ken Kesey in *One Flew over the Cuckoo's Nest* (1962) – the jailhouse is replaced by the asylum as the only place in which any kind of salvation and personal integrity can be retrieved.

The morning after the reading, Ginsberg received a card from Lawrence Ferlinghetti, saying – in a clear and deliberate echo of Ralph Waldo Emerson's congratulatory letter to Walt Whitman after reading the latter's *Leaves of Grass* (1855) – 'I greet you at the beginning of a great career. When do I get the manuscript?' Ferlinghetti (b. 1919) was a New Yorker who had served in the naval reserve and witnessed the horrific scenes in Nagasaki, where he had been sent soon after the atomic bomb that killed around forty thousand people had been dropped. Following study at the University of North Carolina and Columbia, he moved to France and studied for a PhD at the Sorbonne. In Paris in the late 1940s, he met Kenneth Rexroth and was impressed enough by Rexroth's tales of the San Francisco poetry

---

[5] Henry David Thoreau, 'Resistance to Civil Government' ('Civil Disobedience'), in *Walden and Civil Disobedience* (Harmondsworth, England: Penguin, 1983), p. 398.

community to head west on his return to the United States. Having also encountered George Whitman, a fellow American who ran an English-language bookshop on Paris's Left Bank that was modelled on Shakespeare & Co., bookstore to the expatriate 1920s Lost Generation, Ferlinghetti (initially with Peter Martin as partner) opened his own shop in San Francisco.

Thus, by the time of the Six Gallery reading, Ferlinghetti was an odd combination of artist and businessman; not only a poet but also owner of City Lights, a paperback bookstore located on Columbus Avenue which had just branched into publishing with the appearance of his own *Pictures of the Gone World*. The collection was issued as number one in the City Lights Pocket Poets series and was followed by volumes from Rexroth (*Thirty Spanish Poems of Love and Exile*) and Kenneth Patchen (*Poems of Humor and Protest*). The Pocket Poets series was the ideal product to capitalize on the sense of poetry reading being a popular activity for the disaffected young. The books were cheap, small and with their black-and-white covers – instantly recognizable – an ideal combination for a Beat audience with low income, commitment to cheap travel, and a strong sense of community. *Howl and Other Poems*, which appeared in 1956 as volume 4, was a book perfectly designed to satisfy these requirements, containing not only the title poem but also an introduction by William Carlos Williams – a stamp of authority that indicated that Ginsberg was a serious poet – and a selection of the best of Ginsberg's new work which included 'Sunflower Sutra', 'America' and 'A Supermarket in California', a witty homage to Walt Whitman written during Ginsberg's time in Berkeley in 1955.

The 'Howl' obscenity trial

The Six Gallery reading had made Ginsberg a local celebrity in San Francisco, but – with only a thousand copies of *Howl* printed – it was evident that Ferlinghetti was not planning on a national bestseller. Even before publication, City Lights was concerned that the book's content might run foul of the censors and Ferlinghetti took the precaution of enlisting the backing of the American Civil Liberties Union in case of trouble. Ginsberg, too, was forced to tone down his language during readings in early 1956. In any case, following the death of his mother – which would inspire him to write 'Kaddish' (1961), his next great long poem – he left the country to visit William Burroughs in Tangier (Kerouac was already there) and then to settle at the 'Beat Hotel' in the rue Git-le-Coeur in Paris, where many of the founding Beats would establish an international wing in the late 1950s and early 1960s. It was only with the printing of the second edition – with Ginsberg already gone – that trouble flared: the book had been printed in England and US Customs seized five hundred copies en route to California, declared the contents obscene and proceeded to arrest Ferlinghetti and a City Lights assistant. Despite spending a short spell in jail, Ferlinghetti was delighted, realizing that the press coverage of the seizure and subsequent trial was better publicity than anything he could have conceived. With several leading academics willing to testify to the poem's worth, the charges were thrown out in October 1957 and the judge declared that 'Howl' was of 'redeeming social importance'. The trial attracted the interest of the national media and both *Time* and *Life* ran features, virtually guaranteeing the success of the book, and the establishment of Ginsberg as the leading voice of the new poetry movement and of City Lights as an enlightened and daring new press. Several subsequent efforts to censor publication of writings by the Beat Generation – most notably when the *Chicago Review* fell foul of the trustees of the University of Chicago when it decided to publish extracts from Burroughs's *Naked Lunch* in a special issue devoted to the San Francisco Renaissance – only helped to spread the word that a new form of writing, dedicated to overthrowing tired establishment views, was on the streets.

On the road at last

The 'Howl' obscenity trial concluded on 3 October 1957, four weeks after the publication of *On the Road* and six years after Kerouac had typed the first draft onto a single scroll of paper. The key elements of the book − Sal Paradise's friendship with Dean Moriarty, his trips back and forth across the country and down to Mexico, the search for transcendent experience in jazz and sex and Sal's final rejection of Dean − are so well known that there is no need to examine them here. Anyone with an interest in the Beat Generation should read the novel, rather than a synopsis of it. What is not apparent from the novel − and what was missed by many of the fans and critics of the book at the time of its publication − is the significance of the lengthy delay between composition and publication. First, *On the Road* is an account of the period between 1947 and 1950, and is very much a book about the America of the 1940s, rather than that of the late 1950s when suburbanization, new highways and the coming of the baby boomer generation were creating a landscape barely recognizable as the place that Kerouac describes. Second, Kerouac himself was by now thirty-five years old and looked it − he hardly passed as the young figure of Sal Paradise or of Dean Moriarty, whom many readers assumed to be the 'Kerouac' figure in the novel.

More importantly, the half dozen years that had elapsed since the first writing had seen Kerouac forced to compromise his vision of spontaneous prose. After a series of false dawns, *On the Road* was finally accepted by Viking Press, on the condition that Kerouac edited his text to the satisfaction of Malcolm Cowley (1898–1989), a veteran of the Lost Generation's time in Paris, who had written a classic account of those years in *Exile's Return* (1934) and who edited Viking's *Portable* [William] *Faulkner* (1946), an imaginatively reconstructed anthology that played a sizable part in consolidating Faulkner's reputation and bringing him the Nobel Prize for Literature in 1949. With his immersion in radical modernism, Cowley was, therefore, by no means the old fuddy-duddy depicted by Kerouac and by many writers of Beat history. Despite his background, however, Cowley was also aware of the commercial requirements of a major publisher and argued that, as it stood, *On the Road* was not publishable, a point that Kerouac refuted for several years, before finally and reluctantly agreeing to make revisions. Cowley was probably right in his belief that the original text – typed out as a single paragraph and including many sections that had little apparent relevance to the narrative's central strand – would not have found a market and he continued to push Kerouac to revise his other works in similar fashion if he wanted Viking to publish them. Kerouac, however, along with Ginsberg, felt that the version that appeared in 1957 (which even included Cowley's own revisions, some made after Kerouac had seen the proofs) failed to capture the rhythms and – most importantly – the spontaneity of the original, and refused ever fully to forgive his editor for what had happened.

Whatever Kerouac believed about its final form, the success of *On the Road* took the notoriety of the Beat Generation to a level that even the 'Howl' trial could not have achieved alone. To his many admirers, he was soon the 'King of the Beats'; to his detractors, he was a threat to all the values held dear by conservative America. For Kerouac himself, the popularity of *On the Road* was double-edged, and he felt that his other works, many of which he considered superior, were unjustly neglected. In the following chapter, I turn to a selection of these books in order to assess the significance of 'The Legend of Duluoz', the life work of which *On the Road* is just one section.

4

Jack Kerouac: 'King of the Beats'

The attention paid to *On the Road* has tended to deflect attention from Jack Kerouac's other writings. While most are now in print (a state of affairs that was often not the case in the years immediately following his death), they remain relatively unknown. The effect of this imbalance is twofold: First, the full range of Kerouac's formal experimentations is not apparent to readers familiar solely with the published version of *On the Road*. Kerouac was a member of the cultural avant-garde that represented both a late flowering of modernism and a harbinger of the postmodernist fascination with popular styles which would come to dominate much of the art of the 1960s and beyond. His books are written in distinct, often very different styles, designed to capture the 'sounds' of whatever subject matter – Bebop, the road, childhood dreams, etc. – is represented in the narrative. Second, *On the Road* becomes detached from the 'one vast book . . . written on the run'[1] that comprises what Kerouac labelled 'The Legend of Duluoz'. Within this vast fictional autobiography, *The Town and the City* (1950), *Doctor Sax* (1959), *Maggie Cassidy* (1959), *Visions of Gerard* (1963) and *Vanity of Duluoz* (1968) serve as novelistic transformations of Kerouac's own early experiences in Lowell, Massachusetts and at college, whereas *On the Road* (1957), *The Dharma Bums* (1958), *Tristessa* (1960), *Visions of Cody* (1973), *The Subterraneans* (1958), *Big Sur* (1962),

---

[1] Jack Kerouac, *Big Sur* (London: Panther, 1984), p. 5.

Desolation Angels (1965) and *Satori in Paris* (1966) are representations of his adventures among the hipsters and beats of post-war America and (occasionally) beyond.

Kerouac's nostalgic vision of America

If there is one mood that characterizes the entire 'Legend', it is the nostalgic yearning for the pre-war days 'when full-grown men, hands deep in jacket pockets, used to go whistling down the street unnoticed by anybody and noticing no one themselves'.[2] Kerouac's narrators look back to an age of innocence, of 'not knowing' the horrors that they believe confront the modern world, but can only do so as a kind of symbolic compensation for their own knowledge that America has unleashed the atom bomb, is living through the 'Plastic Fifties'[3] and has bred what his narrators perceive as the 'illiterate generation' of the 1960s. Kerouac's lament is that he can no longer recognize Americans 'as people any more';[4] his (in the light of *On the Road*, ironic) loathing for the motor car and for the 'rancid blight'[5] of television, with 'everybody looking at the same thing and thinking the same thing at the same time',[6] alongside his insistence on his own outsider status as 'Franco-American' or son of French Canadian immigrants, dictates that he eulogizes a childhood fixed in the local rather than the national community, even while he recognizes (in a contradiction that

[2] Jack Kerouac, *Vanity of Duluoz* (St Albans, England: Granada, 1982), p. 9.
[3] Jack Kerouac, *Maggie Cassidy* (St Albans, England: Granada, 1982), pp. 9, 48.
[4] Kerouac, *Vanity of Duluoz*, p. 9.
[5] Jack Kerouac, *Visions of Gerard* (New York: McGraw-Hill, 1976), p. 31.
[6] Jack Kerouac, *The Dharma Bums* (St Albans, England: Granada, 1982), p. 31.

is typical of Kerouac's narratives) that Lowell is a stultifying environment that must be escaped.

In *Memory Babe*, the most exhaustive biography of Kerouac that has yet been published, Gerald Nicosia has commented on the significance of Kerouac's ethnic origins. For Nicosia,

> Growing up in a French-Canadian colony (itself a hybrid culture) separated by choice from the American melting pot, Kerouac came by double vision early . . . This learning was reinforced by a strongly mystical Catholic education, itself immeasurable aided by Jack's kinship with a childhood saint [his brother, Gerard], whose presence grew increasingly vital after his death.[7]

Nicosia is correct to focus on the location of the Kerouac family on the margins of dominant American culture: in many ways, they were the archetypal immigrant family, distanced from the 'norms' of American life by a combination of language, religion and custom. Kerouac constantly offers reminders of these cultural differences, in particular through his willingness to insert French phrases into his writing and, most importantly, in the degree to which Catholicism (and a Catholic sense of guilt about sexual desire and activity) shapes his consciousness, even during his flirtations with Buddhism. Nevertheless, another aspect of the quintessential immigrant narrative (at least, as it functioned from the mid-nineteenth to the mid-twentieth century) is also at work here in the manner that Kerouac and his fictional self-representations are expected to move away from these roots, and from the lifestyles of their parents, and become 'Americanized'. Early sections of the 'Legend' emphasize the possibility of integration via education – Jacky Duluoz's scholarships to Horace Mann and Columbia – in a narrative that, while never entirely abandoning

---

[7] Gerald Nicosia, *Memory Babe* (Harmondsworth, England: Penguin, 1986), p. 502.

origins, certainly subsumes them beneath the ambitions codified in the American Dream. Similarly, in Kerouac's first published novel, *The Town and the City*, it is the *American* qualities of the Martin family (who live in the small New England town of Galloway) that are pitted against the evils of the big city. The novel deploys an American fable with roots stretching back at least to Thomas Jefferson, in which the smallholder and local businessman represent an idealized democratic legacy struggling against corrupt corporate metropolitan powers. The composition and form of *The Town and the City*, 'written in tradition of long work and revision from 1946 to 1948, three years'[8], also, in themselves, display a commitment to the myth of the American Dream of success via hard work and persistence, while the character of Peter Martin is expected to use his college education to secure rich pickings as an insurance salesman.

Kerouac, of course, went on to reject this path, developing his form of spontaneous prose as a counter to the process of disciplined self-improvement via a combination of hard work and steady acquisition most famously marked out in Benjamin Franklin's *Autobiography*. His alternative, however, depends upon the redeployment of another American narrative, this time drawn from the canonical literary challenge to American ideological orthodoxy. In *Vanity of Duluoz*, a late novel constructed as a long letter to Kerouac's third wife and, in many ways, his most autobiographical work, he explains that 'Tom Wolfe . . . just woke me up to America as a Poem instead of America as a place to struggle around and sweat in.'

The format of the novel, written for 'wifey', imitates Herman Melville's poem, 'Bridegroom Dick', addressed to 'old wifie', while the narrator is conscious of overlooking 'Thoreau's woods' while he writes and of his position as an Emersonian

---

[8] Jack Kerouac, *Lonesome Traveller* (St Albans, England: Granada, 1982), p. 11.

THOMAS WOLFE

Although little read now, Thomas Wolfe (1900–38) was one of the most significant American writers of the first half of the twentieth century. In the 1930s, Wolfe was often favourably compared with Ernest Hemingway as a writer able to capture the essence of American life. Wolfe's four major novels – *Look Homeward, Angel* (1929), *Of Time and the River* (1935), *The Web and the Rock* (1939) and *You Can't Go Home Again* (1940) – served as prototypes for Kerouac's project of turning his life into fiction. Wolfe's childhood in Asheville, North Carolina was considerably more affluent than Kerouac's working-class origins in Lowell, but his eagerness to escape the oppressive provincialism that he sensed in Asheville resulted in a life divided between travelling and living in New York which anticipated Kerouac's own. Wolfe's fiction – like Kerouac's – is generally about himself, tracing his life from the innocence of a southern childhood through his college education to his experiences as a writer. His passages depicting the American landscape of the 1930s (often described as it flashes before his eyes through the window of a train) serve both as inspiration and model for sections of *On the Road* where Sal describes the experience of seeing the country disappear behind him as he and Dean race across the continent. In many ways, Wolfe's (near obsessive) interest in the workings of memory and his quest for meaning in life act as precursors to Kerouac's 'Legend of Duluoz'. Wolfe was also instrumental in shaping Kerouac's ideas about spontaneous prose. He also wrote at speed, with little revision, although he experienced pressure from editors to revise his works for publication which foreshadowed the insistence of Malcolm Cowley and others that *On the Road* be revised and rewritten several times before it was published.

Kerouac's first published novel, *The Town and the City*, is highly reminiscent of Wolfe in both style and content. It is possible that the large Martin family (in which Kerouac's persona is spread across several brothers) was inspired by Wolfe's own treatment of his childhood as the youngest of eight children. Subsequently,

THOMAS WOLFE (cont.)

however, Kerouac's attitude to Wolfe's prose style – if not his books' content – became more equivocal and he rejected what he perceived to be the conventional structuring of Wolfe's language, replacing it with his own form of spontaneous prose.

'nonconformist', unable to 'recognise myself as a real member of something called the human race'.[9] In other words, as Kerouac seems keen to stress, to be a non-conformist also requires a tradition rooted in American (literary) history.

If Kerouac's position as 'King of the Beats' is properly to be understood, it is essential to consider the 'Legend' as a whole. Kerouac's notion of Beat, as articulated in an article for *Playboy* in 1959, combines a coupling of the Catholic sense of 'beatitude' with an awareness of his ancient Breton ancestors' defence of their independence; memories of the 'fantastically loud' parties that his father threw in Lowell in the 1930s and of his own childhood fantasies from the same period; and memories of the comic strips and movies (Laurel and Hardy, the Marx Brothers, etc.) of the time. Kerouac insists that the energy, joy and compassion inherent to all of the above form the basis for the Beat Generation's own quest for 'kicks'. This past, as much as the energy found in the Bebop of Kerouac's early adulthood (that is, the source most commonly associated with the Beat Generation), is represented in the opening sections of the 'Legend' and these should be read alongside novels like *On the Road* and *The Subterraneans* if a full appreciation of Kerouac's intentions is to be achieved.[10] In its entirety, however, the

[9] Kerouac, *Vanity of Duluoz*, pp. 9, 85–6, 9.
[10] Jack Kerouac, '*Beatific*: The Origins of the Beat Generation', in *The Portable Jack Kerouac*, edited by Ann Charters (New York: Penguin, 1996), pp. 565–73.

'Legend' cannot be discussed fruitfully within a book dedicated to a reading of the Beat Generation as a whole. Rather than offering what would necessarily be very brief readings of each novel, I will, therefore, trace some of the formal and thematic patterns and variations in Kerouac's fiction through slightly longer analyses of five books that are representative of various stages of the 'Legend'. Following discussion of *Doctor Sax* and *Maggie Cassidy*, novels that represent two stages of Duluoz's childhood and youth in Lowell, I will turn to *The Subterraneans*, *The Dharma Bums* and *Big Sur* as examples of three very different moments in Kerouac's Beat history.

Experimental memories of childhood, 1: *Doctor Sax*

Chronologically, *Doctor Sax* is the second novel in the 'Legend', following on from *Visions of Gerard*, Kerouac's fictionalized memoir of his brother, who died age nine when Kerouac was four. *Doctor Sax* recounts Duluoz's late boyhood and the onset of adolescence, blending historical detail with fantasy to suggest the mind of a child already dreaming of the possibilities of life beyond Lowell. Calling attention to the experimental formal processes involved in this approach, Gerald Nicosia has suggested that, 'if John Barth is correct in assuming that the true postmodernist writer has "one foot in fantasy, one in objective reality", then *Doctor Sax* was the first postmodern novel in America'.[11] Nicosia does not develop the point, but it can provide a valuable entry to understanding the radical nature of the book, even if it is not hard to find historical precursors in the nineteenth century, such as Edgar Allan Poe's *The Narrative of Arthur Gordon Pym*, Nathaniel Hawthorne's *The Scarlet Letter* and

[11] Nicosia, *Memory Babe*, p. 393.

Herman Melville's *The Confidence Man*, all of which satisfy the rather narrow definition of postmodernism from Barth that is used to support Nicosia's assertion. Indeed, it is worth pointing out that Kerouac's willingness to blend the factual and the fantastic in this manner is one way in which he can be placed within a canonical American literary genealogy.

While Nicosia's own allusion to postmodernism is limited, it is possible to understand the radical scope of Kerouac's artistic avant-gardism by reading *Doctor Sax* as an exemplar of the wider criteria for postmodernism offered by the literary and cultural critic Fredric Jameson. Jameson calls attention to one

> Fundamental feature of all . . . postmodernisms . . . namely, the effacement in them of the older (essentially high-modernist) frontier between high culture and so-called mass or commercial culture, and the emergence of new kinds of texts infused with the forms, categories and contents of that very Culture Industry so passionately denounced by all the ideologues of the modern.[12]

Doctor Sax anticipates the texts outlined by Jameson in its incorporation of the comic strip and radio figure Lamont Cranston (alias, 'The Shadow') and the 'mass' culture worlds of horror movies, W.C. Fields and popular fiction, alongside a structure drawn from *The Scarlet Letter* and the mystical language of French Canadian Catholicism, in a narrative whose major themes include the threat posed to local culture by the invasion of national and international voices made available by the still relatively young technologies of the cinema, radio and comic strip. While Kerouac recognizes that these technologies challenge the very survival of his hometown values, he also embraces them as invaluable components of his own storytelling techniques.

[12] Fredric Jameson, 'Postmodernism, or the Cultural Logic of Late Capitalism', *New Left Review*, 146 (1984), p. 54.

It would probably be going too far to suggest that *Doctor Sax* is a postmodern novel in the manner of, for example, the works of Thomas Pynchon or Kurt Vonnegut in the 1960s and beyond. There are many passages, especially in the opening chapter, that can easily be identified as Kerouac's 'personal' style. On the other hand, there is no sense that these sections are privileged over others equally integral to the narrative. The description of the arrival of Count Condu is a pastiche of 1930s vampire movies; the dialogue of the Doctor Sax/Old Bull Balloon pool game recreates the world of W.C. Fields; Amadeus Baroque's discovery of the 'curliqueing yellow sheaf of papers'[13] and his consequent 'writing' of the novel *Doctor Sax* is (as Nicosia and others have pointed out) a reconstruction of Hawthorne's purported discovery of the old piece of cloth and accompanying history in the Salem Custom House that precipitates his writing of *The Scarlet Letter*. Significantly, Kerouac was staying in William Burroughs's apartment in Mexico City while he wrote parts of the book and – with the hindsight possible from knowledge of Burroughs's own thematic concerns – it is possible to trace many similarities between *Doctor Sax* and Burroughs's work. The novel also includes a section of poetry, parodies of other prose styles and, most importantly, the integration of the comic strip into its structure *and* into the lives and consciousnesses of the characters, so that the children enact the fantasies of the comics. Ultimately, however, Kerouac's purpose seems at odds with what Jameson describes as postmodernism's inseparability from the 'degraded' world of multinational capitalism.[14] Instead, Kerouac's methodology also mimics the transformative reworkings of the drab working-class world that Jameson describes in his analysis of

[13] Jack Kerouac, *Doctor Sax* (London: Panther Books, 1984), p. 120. The Count Condu and Doctor Sax/Old Bull Balloon passages are pp. 19–24 and 26–7, respectively.
[14] Jameson, 'Postmodernism', p. 71.

earlier artistic engagements with modernity, such as Vincent Van Gogh's *Peasant Shoes*, in Kerouac's case deploying the colours of the modern world to transform the drab space of 1930s Lowell into a utopian fantasy that serves as a dramatic counterpart to the 'Plastic Fifties' in which Kerouac is writing.

There is, of course, an unintended irony in this process that is indicative of a wider tension within Kerouac's fiction. In *Kerouac's Town*, a memoir of Lowell published two years after Kerouac's death, Barry Gifford suggests that the town's 'adult chill could only be enlivened by the fantasy of the child's eye'.[15] This process is only possible, however, via the intrusion of the comic strip world of 'The Shadow' and *Star Western*, produced for national consumption, as the narrator knows, in a 'redbrick building, somehow sooty, with big sign STREET & SMITH on it, in white, dirty white, now Street & Smith Street in the downtown section of Pittsburgh New York'.[16] While seeming to want to describe a local, pre-war community as the idyllic and archetypal American small town, Kerouac is compelled to invoke the output of the city. Without this, he can see only poverty and class and racial conflict in a strictly ethnically divided community. The incorporation of mass culture, cited by Jameson as an inevitable and lamentable consequence of the triumph of multinational capitalism, serves, ironically, for Kerouac as the best way to cling to the innocent outlook of childhood in the face of the 'horrors' (the Second World War and the atom bomb, but also the transformation of America by the 1950s and, most importantly, his sense of his own corruption) that have come between him and his youth.

Ultimately, *Doctor Sax* is a novel that marks the end of the young Duluoz's innocence and an initiation into adulthood that

---

[15] Quoted in John Tytell, *Naked Angels* (New York: McGraw-Hill, 1976), p. 190.
[16] Kerouac, *Doctor Sax*, p. 179.

enacts Kerouac's perennial return to Catholic guilt. In the final chapters, Jacky Duluoz and Sax race around Lowell, in scenes that integrate all the styles invoked within the novel in a surrealistic maelstrom of life, movies, comics, ancient Indian myths and dreams. But because this transformation of reality is in itself perceived as a 'triumph', it invokes the narrator's Catholic sense of guilt and compels him to look 'down to face my horror, my tormentor, my mad-face demon mirror of myself'. Earlier in the book, Duluoz recollects that he heard the news of his dog's death 'at precisely the moment in my life when I was lying in bed finding out that my tool had sensations in the tip . . . Beauty [Jacky's dog] dies the night I discover sex'.[17] Kerouac puns (rather obviously, perhaps) on the dog's death to stress what Sax has revealed to Jacky – that childhood can never be reclaimed once maturity brings awareness of the 'sin' inherent to sexual activity. In the end, as with so many of Kerouac's books, Catholic guilt becomes the dominant voice, undermining the author's efforts to recreate boyhood innocence (in his fiction) with a reminder of the inescapable realities (for Kerouac) of religious doctrine.

Experimental memories of childhood, 2: *Maggie Cassidy*

Bruce Cook, one of the first critics to take Kerouac seriously as a writer, has argued that the 'Lowell novels are not nearly as good [as the Road novels]. They lack excitement, drive, intensity, focus – all the finest qualities of Kerouac's writing.'[18] This view has been shared by many readers, but even a cursory glance

---

[17] Ibid., pp. 210, 108.
[18] Bruce Cook, *The Beat Generation* (New York: Charles Scribner's, 1971), p. 78.

at *Doctor Sax* should refute such a harsh judgment, since the terms Cook identifies as Kerouac's strengths are ideally suited to describing the novel's structure and content. Likewise, *Maggie Cassidy*, written a few months later and picking up the Legend where *Sax* leaves off, is one of the most striking elements of the Kerouac canon, deploying the narratorial pattern of the earlier novel – a disillusioned writer looking back from the 1950s to the innocence of the 1930s – but developing a very different formal approach to represent the teenage Duluoz's new interests.

Unsurprisingly, Kerouac realized that the comic strip fantasies of *Doctor Sax* would be inappropriate to his account of the transition to sexual maturity. Instead, *Maggie Cassidy* appears to represent events more factually, only occasionally (largely in the opening chapters) calling attention to the significance of movie stars such as Boris Karloff, Tyrone Power and Charlie Chaplin as inspirations for Jacky and his friends' fantasies. One exception to this realism is the transformation of a black-and-white world into colour, borrowed from *The Wizard of Oz*, a movie that Kerouac had seen while writing *Doctor Sax*. The change takes place at the moment that Jacky meets Maggie and it is notable that the early descriptions of her house and its surrounds contain a symbol-packed (and very sentimental) romanticism that contrasts sharply with the representations of the grim realities of a declining industrial town that surround them. On the whole, the novel takes a critical look at Duluoz's experiences of life in Lowell and, later, New York, exposing the gulf between the fantasy worlds of Hollywood and Street & Smith comics and the environment that exists beyond their realm. *Maggie Cassidy* describes the manner in which Jacky's relationship with Maggie sets in motion the loss of sexual and spiritual innocence that will culminate in Jack (no longer Jacky) returning to Lowell three years later as a 'man', whose 'adventurous education' of travel, work and football now marks him as an outsider who remains 'poised at the gate', unable to remove

Maggie's symbolic (and very real) 'thick rubber girdle' that thwarts his sexual desires.[19]

Change is a central theme of the novel: at one point, before Jacky departs for New York, the narrator comments that 'everything went on as usual in the city itself – except that it was always changing, like me'. The message of the concluding chapters, however, is that the pace of change is not uniform. In Lowell, transformation is barely perceptible, and the narrator's confession that 'I had little knowledge of the world I lived in'[20] epitomizes the mood of the small town. Only one shop in Lowell stocks the *New York Times* and it is virtually impossible for the inhabitants of a small New England factory town to begin to imagine what New York is really like or, as Maggie discovers when she attends Kerouac's school dance, to comprehend what they encounter.

Maggie's arrival in New York marks the climax of the novel and involves the clash of two cultures. Maggie is constructed as both a representative of the natural world and of the small-town American ideal and, unsurprisingly, is humiliated by the women transformed by 'sorceries of powder' who represent Jacky's artificial big-city companions. Comically, Jacky pictures himself as already belonging to their world, 'like a Cary Grant', and tries to acquire a suntan, with the result that 'the lamp burned and gave me a terrible lobster red face for the ball'. In attempting to simulate the glamour of the movies, he only manages to destroy his natural 'Greek athletic hero' good looks.[21]

The self-mockery of the above passage is characteristic of *Maggie Cassidy* as a whole. In a novel that becomes increasingly critical both of the limitations of Lowell and of the excesses of New York, the tone is generally sad and reflective, unlike the

[19] Kerouac, *Maggie Cassidy*, p. 171.
[20] Ibid., pp. 135, 148.
[21] Ibid., pp. 159, 126.

slapstick yet serious conclusion to *Doctor Sax*. Life in New York exposes Duluoz to a dilemma from which he can no longer escape: he cannot retreat into the comic-strip world of his youth, since he now understands what lies behind it; on the other hand, the reality of life in Lowell is a cycle of drudgery made worse by his knowledge of the world of the big city and by the loss of Maggie. The narrator is aware that the only route left unexplored is the road west and the search for other heroes that this will entail – a point that, in its anticipation of Dean Moriarty and life on the road, further illustrates the links between respective segments of 'The Legend of Duluoz'.

The essentials of spontaneous prose

Although *Maggie Cassidy* lacks the artistic audacity of *Doctor Sax*, its formal elements (in particular, the long, breathless sentences with which Kerouac describes New York) are representative of the style that is more often associated with his 'Beat' or 'jazz' novels, and which he extended in *The Subterraneans*, written a few months after *Maggie Cassidy* in October 1953. The early 1950s were the years in which, having decided to reject the formal structures employed in *The Town and the City*, Kerouac developed what he labelled 'spontaneous prose'. He applied this approach to the first draft of *On the Road* and, although that novel went through numerous revisions at the behest of editors and publishers before its publication in 1957, used it in the composition of the remainder of his oeuvre. Kerouac outlined the key components of his methodology in an essay (or, more accurately, a series of brief notes) titled 'Essentials of Spontaneous Prose', written at the insistence of Allen Ginsberg and William Burroughs in 1953, shortly after he had completed *The Subterraneans*.

'Essentials of Spontaneous Prose' is an invaluable guide to Kerouac's compositional processes. Under the headings 'SET-UP',

'PROCEDURE', 'METHOD', 'SCOPING', 'LAG IN PROCEDURE', 'TIMING', 'CENTER OF INTEREST', 'STRUCTURE OF WORK' and 'MENTAL STATE', he outlines both the conditions necessary for writing successfully in this way and the desired result. First, it is necessary to set the object of study 'before the mind, either in reality, as in sketching . . . or . . . in the memory'. The writer must then create 'undisturbed', since any interruption will result in disruption of the 'purity of speech', drawing on the breath-determined rhythms of jazz to construct flowing sentences unbroken by the 'false colons and timid usually needless commas' of standard English. The key to spontaneous prose is – as the name implies – that it must be put down without 'pause to think of proper word' and should be composed 'in semi-trance . . . allowing subconscious to admit in own uninhibited interesting necessary and so "modern" language what conscious art would censor, and write excitedly, swiftly, with writing-or-typing cramps, in accordance with laws of orgasm'.[22] 'Essentials of Spontaneous Prose' codifies what is probably apparent from a reading of Kerouac's fiction; that is, he is drawing upon a combination of Transcendentalism (here, in particular, Walt Whitman's calls to write freely from and about the self), Bebop jazz (in which improvisation draws the musicians further and further away from the original object or melody in a process of individual and collective self-discovery) and the modernist stream-of-consciousness or trance writing techniques of Gertrude Stein and (explicitly in Kerouac's essay) William Carlos Williams and W.B. Yeats.

What it conceals – apart from the well-known inspiration that Kerouac drew from Neal Cassady's confidence-man spontaneous narratives – is that Kerouac is aware that this process takes

[22] Jack Kerouac, 'Essentials of Spontaneous Prose', in *The Portable Jack Kerouac*, pp. 484–5.

STREAM OF CONSCIOUSNESS WRITING

The importance that many Beats attached to spontaneity in composition was not a new idea. Earlier in the twentieth century, writers such as Gertrude Stein (1874–1946), William Butler Yeats (1865–1939), James Joyce (1882–1941), Virginia Woolf (1882–1941) and William Faulkner (1897–1962) had all experimented with forms of stream-of-consciousness writing. The term was first used by the Harvard psychologist William James (brother of the novelist Henry James) in *The Principles of Psychology* (1890) and refers to the way in which characters' thoughts and feelings are allowed to flow in apparently random order, without any attempt to arrange them chronologically or within other conventional narrative structures. For a writer such as Stein, the process was shaped by the influence of Cubism and its effort to attach equal importance to all parts of the canvas – or, in the case of the author, to every word. While there are major differences in the respective spontaneity of the compositional processes of these authors, their legacy is clear in much of Kerouac's more experimental prose, such as elements of *Visions of Cody* (see especially the 'Joan Rawshanks in the Fog' section), and in 'Old Angel Midnight', a piece that Kerouac described as resembling Joyce's *Finnegans Wake* (1939) but which also bears clear indebtedness to Stein's experiments with sound.

years of practice to master: many of his acquaintances have reminisced that Kerouac was rarely seen without a notebook and that he spent thousands of hours sitting refining his 'sketching' techniques before deploying them in constructing 'The Legend of Duluoz'.[23]

---

[23] See, for example, John Clellon Holmes's *Go* (1952), in which Paul Hobbes (Holmes) observes Gene Pasternak (Kerouac) 'sitting at a table by the window with cooling coffee and a notebook before him, in which he was writing leisurely'. John Clellon Holmes, *Go* (New York: Thunder's Mouth Press, 1988), p. 250.

Kerouac and race

This absence of attention to the training necessary to work spontaneously has been shared by recent critics who have called attention to what they see as the racism inherent to Kerouac's methodology. Overlooking this apprenticeship – as well as his indebtedness to Transcendentalism's emphasis on spontaneity – they have accused Kerouac of imagining African American consciousness in primitivist terms, as something *necessarily* spontaneous and incapable of assimilating to (white) structures of civilization. Both Jon Panish and Peter Townsend are uncomfortable with the manner in which white Beat writers such as Ginsberg and Kerouac aligned themselves with African American jazz, Panish being especially judgmental of Kerouac's novels.

CHARLIE PARKER

While Kerouac had an impressive knowledge of jazz and was enthusiastic about many musicians working in a range of styles, he singled out the Bebop alto saxophonist Charlie 'Yardbird' Parker – more commonly, just 'Bird' – (1920–55) as the great jazz soloist and as a kind of artistic blood brother. Parker was raised in Kansas City and started to learn the sax at age eleven. Although – as with the great Delta blues guitarist, Robert Johnson – innumerable stories are told about his early days as a musician (and most are probably untrue), it seems that, like Johnson in his early days, Parker was a poor player and was repeatedly thrown off stage by other musicians. His response was to practise incessantly, developing an extraordinary technical mastery of his instrument, so that he could play complex compositions in any key. By the time that he headed for New York in 1939, Parker was already experimenting with revolutionary sounds made from unusual chord substitutions and dazzlingly fast improvised passages that coupled his technical mastery with a highly individualistic tone.

CHARLIE PARKER (*cont.*)

Although Bird was playing regular gigs in the city from 1939, his ideas only became codified as 'Bebop' in 1942 during late-night sessions at Minton's in Harlem, where – along with musicians including guitarist Charlie Christian, trumpeter Dizzy Gillespie, drummer Max Roach and pianist Thelonious Monk – he developed a small group routine based on complex improvisations that pushed the musicians to their limit and produced arrangements that roamed far from their melodic bases. This new sound was deliberately exclusionary: it was a self-conscious rejection of the popular Swing bands of the 1930s and also served as a way of keeping less skilled musicians off the stage.

Although it took several years for Kerouac to be won over by Parker's playing, by 1947 he was Kerouac's favourite jazz musician. Parker's style was appealing to Kerouac because it helped him to consolidate his own ideas about composition. Anticipating the 'sketching' techniques that Kerouac would apply to his most noteworthy writings from the early 1950s, Parker used his years of dedication to mastering his craft as the backdrop to ever more daring improvisational passages, starting from a simple theme, occasionally returning to it, but trusting his impulses to lead him where they would. Without that training, the results would have been chaotic and near impossible to listen to; with it, they suggested previously unimaginable new directions for jazz. Kerouac was already equally dedicated to his craft by the time he started to follow Bird, and it was precisely that training that enabled him to recognize and transplant Parker's approach from the bandstand to his notebooks.

These compositional overlaps are matched by some uncanny similarities between the characters of the two men. Parker had a phenomenal appetite for alcohol, drugs, women and food and – like Kerouac – was prone to sudden and violent mood swings. By the time that Kerouac started to rave about him, Parker had also spent six months in Camarillo State Hospital in California, recuperating from the effects of several years of excess, including heroin

CHARLIE PARKER (*cont.*)

addiction. Although he managed to remain relatively clean for some time after his return to New York, and recorded many of his finest cuts during this period, his behaviour became increasingly unpredictable and – as a result of his constant need for money for drugs – he would regularly pawn his sax and have to borrow another for the evening's show.

Although Bird was indubitably a superstar of the jazz world by the early 1950s, his fame was as double-edged as Kerouac's a decade later. Both men struggled to meet the demands made by fans and hangers-on who expected them to behave in a particular manner off stage, and both increased their already sizable consumption of drugs and alcohol in attempts to escape from the realities of their condition. Parker died from a bleeding ulcer while watching television in the hotel suite of Nica de Koenigswarter, a member of the Rothschild banking family and fan and patron of many Bebop musicians. Although Parker was aged thirty-four, the coroner famously estimated his age as fifty-five.

Parker is one of the triumvirate of 'tortured' artists who died within a year of one another and became mythologized as father figures of the counterculture. Along with Jackson Pollock and James Dean, he set the mark by which the excesses and early deaths of not only Kerouac and Cassady but also 1960s rock icons such as Jimi Hendrix, Jim Morrison, Brian Jones and Janis Joplin would be measured. But, while his lifestyle is clearly an integral element of his legacy, it is his music and – in the specific context of this book – his influence on Kerouac that is his most significant contribution.

For Panish, Kerouac's version of the great bop saxophonist Charlie Parker is a 'white fantasy of a black self . . . Kerouac uses jazz not only for its ideal of improvisation but also for its status as a music and subculture that is outside what is traditional and accepted.'[24] The argument is hardly original: LeRoi Jones had made much the same point (though not about Kerouac and other Beats, whom he perceived as natural allies of the African American) in his seminal study of jazz and American culture, *Blues People* (1963), when he noted that 'the white bebopper of the forties was as removed from society as the Negroes, but as a matter of choice . . . [The] Negro himself had no choice.'[25] But Panish goes further: discussing Kerouac's 'Essentials of Spontaneous Prose', he argues that Kerouac's writing philosophy depends on equating black consciousness (in the form of the jazz musician) with 'emotions, and life experience' rather than study. Panish ignores Kerouac's own years of training and, implicitly, his knowledge that the jazz musician would have been through the same processes, pointing out that improvising 'cannot be characterized accurately without referring to the kinds of modification of existing material that reflect dedication and rumination rather than pure spontaneous inspiration'. He is also sceptical about Kerouac's claims to be mimicking Bebop in his prose, pointing out that when Kerouac released recordings of himself reading from his novels to a jazz accompaniment they contained more or less verbatim reproductions of the written texts.[26]

In addition to the problems inherent to Panish's position listed above, it is interesting to note that many leading radical black thinkers of the time did not see Kerouac and the other Beats in this way. For example, Jones – a onetime fellow Beat – is more sympathetic to the reasons for and effects of Beat identification with African American culture than Panish's

---

[24] Jon Panish, *The Color of Jazz: Race and Representation in Postwar American Culture* (Jackson: University Press of Mississippi, 1997), p. 57. Also see Peter Townsend, *Jazz in American Culture* (Edinburgh: Edinburgh University Press, 2000).
[25] LeRoi Jones, *Blues People: The Negro Experience in White America and the Music that Developed from It* (New York: William Morrow, 1963), p. 188.
[26] Panish, *The Color of Jazz*, pp. 110, 125, 137–8.

argument would suggest. In *Blues People*, Jones draws attention to the 'aesthetic analogies, persistent similarities of stance that . . . create identifiable relationships' between 'young Negro musicians' and the Beat Generation and other white artists (especially painters like Jackson Pollock), and observes that the relationship between jazz, art and fiction resulted in 'predictable hostility' to all three from traditionalists. Jones stresses the 'cross-fertilization' between genres, noting that the free jazz of the late 1950s has a rapport with other forms of artistic production at the time.[27] This should not be taken, however, to mean that Kerouac's attitudes to race are straightforward. *Maggie Cassidy*, despite being staged largely in Kerouac's white world, contains one significant, highly problematic racial encounter, and *The Subterraneans* – in which the Duluoz character, here named Leo Percepied, has a relationship with the African American Mardou Fox – illustrates that Kerouac had internalized many of his culture's (and his mother's) attitudes to race.

Among the Beat Generation, 1: *The Subterraneans*

In one of the most memorable passages in *Maggie Cassidy*, Duluoz relates his encounter with a 'Negro' runner during an inter-school athletics meet in a race described as between 'warriors of two nations'. The passage is worth quoting at length, since it reveals the conflicting aspects of Kerouac's attitude to race: his fear that 'I was going to be beaten in my city that night by a Negro' being juxtaposed with his awe at his rival's Bebop-like pose:

He was going to play beating drums to my wild alto.

---

[27] Jones, *Blues People*, pp. 233–34.

> We got down on the line, shivering in a sudden cold gust of
> air from the street . . . To my utter astonishment I saw out of
> the corner of my eye the colored boy laid out almost flat on the
> floor in a low slung fantastic starting position, something
> impossibly modern and submarining and subterranean like bop,
> like the new gesture of a generation . . . I flew ahead of my
> Negro, my Jim, eyes half closed so as not to see the horror of
> his black skin at my breast, and hit the tape well ahead but just
> barely beginning to sense his catching up as he too late gathered
> a stunned momentum and knew that he was beaten anyway and
> by the mind.[28]

There is no doubt that Duluoz is fascinated and impressed by
not only the exoticism but also the modernity of his African
American rival, and is possibly envious of a figure already
belonging to a new generation. On the other hand, the deployment of the white literary tradition of Joseph Conrad and Mark
Twain to describe 'my Negro' helps to stress what the narrator
feels to be his mental superiority over his 'Jim'. In the age of the
great African American athlete, Jesse Owen, who won four gold
medals in front of Adolph Hitler at the 1936 Berlin Olympic
Games, Duluoz still believes that it would be a humiliation to be
defeated by the 'Negro Flyer' with his 'reptilian head stuck out
forward to the run' – that is, by a figure that he cannot quite
recognize as human.[29]

In *The Subterraneans*, written in three days (a point that
greatly impressed Ginsberg and Burroughs), Kerouac self-
consciously incorporates the Bebop rhythms of the 'new' generation as the most appropriate way to tell of Percepied's affair
with Mardou, conducted against the backdrop of the new
hipster culture. He pre-empts the idea that Norman Mailer

[28] Kerouac, *Maggie Cassidy*, pp. 89, 85, 90–1.
[29] Ibid., p. 89.

would later propose in 'The White Negro' (1957), his seminal account of the new generation, that in 'this wedding of the white and the black it was the Negro who brought the cultural dowry',[30] but captures the rhythms so effectively that, according to Ginsberg, the prose paraphrasing Mardou's voice (here representative of urban African American cool) 'was the way she spoke, the syntax even, her style of speaking'.[31]

In an evocative early attempt to describe Kerouac's 'blowing' (as per jazz musician) technique,[32] John Tytell explains how the prose in *The Subterraneans*

> is overwhelming in its syncopated insistence on recording all the emotional and philosophical variables. Musically the passage [a description of the affinity the narrator feels with Charlie Parker] builds on improvised digressions as jazz does, using what blues players call 'landmarks', repeated images that help to unify, and 'scat calling', using the voice as instrument. The passage approaches Kerouac's own ideal of the jazz saxophonist, avidly pursuing the inductably ultimate note, always progressively furthering his sound with another association, reaching for and extending an oceanic continuum as if secretly knowing that to cease means to die.[33]

The links between structure and sound in *The Subterraneans* have been well documented: Gerald Nicosia credits Warren Tallman with first pointing out how 'the narrative line follows the brief love-affair between Percepied and Mardou while the improvised details move, as the title would suggest, down into the clutter of their lives among the guilts and shames which

---

[30] Norman Mailer, 'The White Negro', in *Advertisements for Myself* (London: Panther, 1970), p. 273.
[31] Quoted in Tytell, *Naked Angels*, p. 200.
[32] Kerouac, 'Essentials of Spontaneous Prose', p. 484.
[33] Tytell, *Naked Angels*, p. 199.

come up from the subterranean depths to steal their love from them. The truth is in the improvisation.' Likewise, Robert A. Hipkiss has argued that the complexity of Kerouac's language creates 'a remarkable book . . . in which the spontaneity of style is largely responsible for the strength of its effect'.[34]

As with Kerouac's other protagonists, however, Percepied (despite his feel for modern, urban culture) is undone by his own shortcomings and, in particular, his inability to unshackle himself from his small-town racial bigotry. His descriptions of Charlie Parker recognize the musician's genius but – echoing the encounter with the African American athlete in *Maggie Cassidy* – focus on the near Uncle-Tom-like qualities of humility, physical power and kindness in Parker as a means to stress the narrator's own prowess as an artist. The ambivalent attitude to African Americans is more fully developed in Percepied's relationship with Mardou, where, ironically, Kerouac uses his imitation of black jazz to expose his own racial prejudices. To apply Mailer's terms from 'The White Negro', the narrator of *The Subterraneans* is 'Hip' in his aptitude for jazz rhythms, but 'Square' in his colour-consciousness, a split that is representative of the conflicted state of many (if not all) of Kerouac's protagonists. In the end, with echoes of *Doctor Sax* and *Maggie Cassidy*, the novel becomes another act of Catholic repentance in the form of 'confession after confession'.[35] Although some attempt is made to link the confessional and Bebop, since both are posited as spontaneous outpourings of deep emotions which take place within controlled environments that place limits on what can be expressed, there is no doubt – as the lengthy passages exploring Percepied's relationship with his mother make clear – that Percepied (like Kerouac) will always choose his mother and her

---

[34] Nicosia, *Memory Babe*, p. 447; Robert A. Hipkiss, *Jack Kerouac: Prophet of the New Romanticism* (Kansas: Regent's Press, 1976), p. 135.
[35] Jack Kerouac, *The Subterraneans* (New York: Grove Press, 1971), p. 5.

Catholic values rather than another woman's bohemianism. In *The Subterraneans*, Percepied's 'faith' in his mother is rewarded by his divine vision of her as an 'angel' when he goes to the San Francisco railyard and cries for the loss of Mardou.[36] By reversing the journey made in *Doctor Sax* – that is, away from his mother's womb – the narrator takes comfort from his regression to a childlike dependency on his parent. Although the narrator claims that it is the pain of losing Mardou that compels him to write the book, he is also aware that the alternative (rejection by his mother) would be intolerable.

Among the Beat Generation, 2: *The Dharma Bums*

Kerouac's own lifelong dependency on his mother ('Mémère') and her hostility to his lovers and to his Beat Generation confrères such as Allen Ginsberg are well known and towards the end of his life he spent increasing amounts of time living with her and adopting her embittered attitude to his onetime friends. In his last years, Kerouac married Stella Sampas, the sister of childhood Lowell buddy Sebastian, and, effectively, became the hard-drinking small-town conservative living close to and inheriting parental values that – had he married 'Maggie Cassidy' rather than going on the road – he could have become decades sooner.

Mémère's shadow also hangs over *The Dharma Bums*, a more authentically West Coast novel than *The Subterraneans*, in which Kerouac transplanted events that had taken place in New York to San Francisco because he feared legal action from 'Mardou'. As so often in the 'Legend', *The Dharma Bums* hinges upon a split between its narrator's desire for adventure and his

[36] Ibid., p. 142.

inbuilt yearning for stability. Thus, although much of the narrative revolves around Kerouac's alter ego Ray Smith's relationship with Japhy Ryder, Ray returns to his family to watch midnight mass on television at Christmas Eve, and Japhy later prophesies Ray's rejection of Buddhism, stating, 'I can just see you on your deathbed kissing the cross like some old Karamazov.'[37]

As with all of Kerouac's books, it would be a mistake to call *The Dharma Bums* 'autobiography'. Although the events that are described – including a recreation of the Six Gallery poetry night where Allen Ginsberg (Alvah Goldbook) first read 'Howl' ('Wail') and Kerouac's meeting and blossoming friendship with Gary Snyder (Japhy Ryder) – correspond closely to the author's own life, Kerouac was never averse to injecting fictional passages to serve symbolic or allegoric purposes. In an essay on Kerouac, published to commemorate his life and writing, William Burroughs also questions the relationship between an author's life and fiction:

> To what extent writers can and do act out their writing in so-called real life, and how useful it is for their craft, are open questions. That is, are you making your universe more like the real universe, or are you pulling the real one into yours?[38]

Many critics have claimed that in *The Dharma Bums* Kerouac went too far in 'novelizing' his life, John Tytell arguing that the book 'suffers from a staged and contrived quality', with 'an almost dogmatic insistence on Western inadequacies', so that the seams of fiction's structure, which Kerouac generally strove to avoid, are all too apparent. For Tytell, and for John Clellon

---

[37] Kerouac, *The Dharma Bums*, p. 145.
[38] William S. Burroughs, 'Remembering Jack Kerouac', in *The Adding Machine (Collected Essays)* (London: John Calder, 1985), p. 176.

Holmes who complained that the 'prose is lax',[39] *The Dharma Bums* shows too many traces of its production, hurriedly written and published to milk the success of *On the Road*.[40]

There is some truth in these assertions: although the writing is never leaden, it lacks the exuberance of the best sections of *Road* or *The Subterraneans* while episodes such as the encounters with a woman preacher and a truck driver are overly formulaic in their efforts to juxtapose American consumer culture with the alternative offered by Japhy. Nevertheless, *The Dharma Bums* – published midway through Eisenhower's second term when an emergent youth culture was showing increasing signs of restlessness in the face of the blandness and conformism of 'official' culture – is a valuable attempt to suggest that another way of life, closely resembling that of the frontiersmen of American myth, remained possible. Whereas Kerouac's prototype western hero, Dean Moriarty, is a 'con-man' whose energies lack direction, Japhy uses his physical and mental resources to pursue specific aims, both for himself and in the hope of inspiring a 'great rucksack revolution' in America. Ray Smith sees him as the epitome of 'truly American optimism',[41] able to live off the land without destroying it and enjoying a relationship with Nature as imagined by the Transcendentalists but apparently lost in the modern world. For Kerouac, Japhy serves as a contemporary Thoreau, who draws upon a combination of Eastern philosophy

[39] Tytell, *Naked Angels*, pp. 171–2; John Clellon Holmes, quoted in Barry Gifford and Lawrence Lee, *Jack's Book* (London: Hamish Hamilton, 1979), p. 244.

[40] There is no doubt that Viking applied pressure on Kerouac to write a sequel to *On the Road*. The publisher refused to bring out any of Kerouac's earlier manuscripts (the eight novels written between the first drafting of *Road* and its publication). It is unlikely, however, that Kerouac offered much resistance, given that he claims in *The Subterraneans* that his goal in writing novels was 'to make a lot of money' (p. 111).

[41] Jack Kerouac, *On the Road* (London: Penguin, 1987), p. 10; idem, *The Dharma Bums*, pp. 72, 150.

and the frontier spirit to expose the hollowness of consumer culture's promises.

Unsurprisingly, perhaps, given *The Dharma Bums'* publication history, there are similarities between it and *On the Road*. Most notably, as with the relationship between Sal and Dean, there is a sizable gulf between Ray and Japhy in terms of background and ambitions. In *The Dharma Bums*, the name 'Ray Smith' locates the narrator even more firmly within the American mainstream than Sal Paradise: like Peter Martin in *The Town and the City*, but in sharp contrast to Jack Duluoz, Sal or Leo Percepied, whose surnames suggest an exotic distance from the WASP mainstream, Ray suggests the embodiment of an 'all-American' identity. The effect is to heighten the sense of rebellion provoked by Smith's conversion to Buddhism and to appeal to the nascent 'beatnik' community of middle-class white youths who want to believe that forms of counter-hegemonic resistance are also available to them despite their conservative heritage.

The America that Kerouac portrays in *The Dharma Bums* is a frighteningly homogenized, consumption-obsessed nation, overshadowed by the 'Red Scare' and governed by a political consensus generally shared by Republicans and Democrats alike. Kerouac anticipates – and, quite clearly, influences – Ken Kesey's *One Flew over the Cuckoo's Nest* (1962) with his description of the United States as an asylum where it would be possible 'to just sit with a hundred other patients in front of a nice television set in a madhouse, where we could be supervised'. Advertising reigns to the extent that a salesman tells Ray how his wife bought a clothes dryer despite 'three hundred and sixty days [sunshine] out of the year' in El Paso. Ray is also reminded of the dark underside of the American Dream when passing 'Alamogordo where the atom bomb was first dropped', an experience that prompts a vision of the words, 'This is the Impossibility of the Existence of Anything.' Ray identifies an almost total lack of freedom behind the illusion of a 'free' society, so that, on the one hand, it is illegal to sleep in the open air, but, on the other, the 'rooftops of Berkeley looked like pitiful living meat from the eternity of the heavens which they feared to face'.[42]

Japhy is constructed as the archetypal Beat hero, an alternative to the corrupted mass culture of American life: he rejects dependency on material goods, living in a small, virtually unfurnished cottage through choice and showing no desire for anything that lacks utility. Furthermore, he pre-empts the 'free love' of the 1960s in his disregard for monogamous American norms, experimenting with what he calls 'Yabyum', a form of group sex in which inhibitions and jealousies are overcome. Significantly, Ray is unwilling to participate, largely as a result of his conservative unwillingness to take his clothes off, or 'do that in front of more than one person, especially with men around'.[43] Smith's background impels him towards a monogamous relationship with a white woman approved of by his mother. Japhy's commitment to the study of Eastern poetry and philosophy and his plan to leave the United States also mark him as free in a way that can never be matched by Kerouac's narrators.

On the other hand, Ray's own construction of Japhy emerges less from what he hears and witnesses than from his (and, as *On the Road* also illustrates, Kerouac's) preconceptions of the western hero. The description of Japhy in his 'rough workingman's clothes', of his home 'in a log cabin in the woods' and of his voice, 'deep and resonant and somehow brave like the voice of oldtime American heroes and orators', is accurate enough, but is drawn from the clichés presented in the Street & Smith comics of Kerouac's youth rather than capturing an 'authentic' western idiom. Although Ray admires Japhy's poetry and studies, he prefers to see him as a reborn Davy Crockett or

[42] Kerouac, *The Dharma Bums*, pp. 89, 114, 95, 29.
[43] Ibid., p. 25.

Abraham Lincoln rather than for what he is, a man rejecting America. All of Ray's descriptions stress Japhy's Americanness, but do so in the very terms that Japhy undermines: Ray's account of Japhy 'singing at the stove like a millionaire' exposes his own small-town capitalist background but seems totally unsuited to a man who claims,

> I admit it, I'm scared of all this American wealth, I'm just an old bhikku and I got nothing to do with all this high standard of living, goddammit, I've been a poor guy all my life and I can't get used to some things.[44]

When Japhy's own views are allowed to surface, they present a figure at odds with the one described by Ray. Japhy has no time for romanticized pop cultural visions of America's past and is more interested in changing its future, since he believes that 'nobody has any fun or believes in anything, especially freedom'. In direct contrast to Ray's eulogies, he claims that 'I didn't feel that I was an American at all, with all that suburban ideal and sex repression and general dreary newspaper gray censorship of all our real human values.' In the greatest irony of all – apparently lost on Ray – Japhy feels the need to abandon America in order to fulfil his potential and discover 'the Dharma'.[45]

When Japhy's prophesy of a 'rucksack revolution' came true a decade later, it was partly inspired by *On the Road* and *The Dharma Bums*. Ironically, both admirers and critics of Kerouac usually failed to distinguish between Sal Paradise and Ray Smith, who are generally observers, and Dean Moriarty and Japhy Ryder, who provide and inspire motion. The opening chapter of *Big Sur* makes Kerouac's distaste for his would-be imitators quite clear and *Vanity of Duluoz* indicates a loathing for the hippie generation who arrived at his house expecting to find

[44] Ibid., pp. 14, 11, 15, 153, 69.
[45] Ibid., pp. 26, 154.

Dean Moriarty. At the other extreme, an influential critic such as Norman Podhoretz could also entirely miss the point of Kerouac's message. For Podhoretz,

> The Bohemianism of the 1950s . . . is hostile to civilization, it worships primitivism, instinct, energy, 'blood'. To the extent that it has intellectual interests at all, they run to mystical doctrines, irrationalist philosophies, and left-wing Reichianism. The only art the new Bohemians have any use for is jazz, mainly of the cool variety. Their predilection for bop language is a way of demonstrating solidarity with the primitive vitality and spontaneity they find in jazz and of expressing contempt for coherent, rational discourse which, being a product of the mind, is in their view a form of death. To be articulate is to admit that you have no feelings (for how can real feelings be expressed in syntactical language?), that you can't respond to anything (Kerouac responds to everything by saying 'Wow!') and that you are probably impotent.[46]

Podhoretz's vitriolic attack is representative of the anti-Beat sentiments that dominated academic and critical responses to the group in the late 1950s. Although he is correct in identifying the Beat celebration of energy and instinct, almost everything else he asserts is inaccurate, succinctly revealing the hegemonic paranoia of an age when FBI Director J. Edgar Hoover saw 'beatniks' as second only to the Soviet Union in their threat to the United States. Podhoretz's criticism – directed specifically at Kerouac and Ginsberg in this essay – misses the point of what the Beat Generation were seeking. Although Kerouac (and his narrators) abandon university and pursue Dean Moriarty and Japhy Ryder because they symbolize a mythic west, his writing draws knowledgeably on a formidable canon of European,

---

[46] Norman Podhoretz, 'The Know-Nothing Bohemians', in *Doings and Undoings* (London: Rupert Hart-Davis, 1965), p. 147.

Eastern and American literature for reference and upon core American values for moral support. In *The Dharma Bums*, Japhy Ryder is a graduate student studying Oriental languages and all his arguments appear entirely 'rational'. Moreover, although Kerouac's prose repeatedly transcends the confines of traditional English grammar, this never obfuscates meaning, as Podhoretz suggests, since – despite their often great length and syntactical complexity – the sentences evolve clearly. The term 'primitive' is, of course, relative and if Podhoretz feels that it is apposite to descriptions of Eastern philosophies and African American music, then this only confirms the conservative prejudice of the American establishment that Kerouac yearns to escape. Ironically, Podhoretz suggests that Kerouac threatens the 'liberal consensus', while much of the 'King of the Beats'' writing only demonstrates his fundamental belief in it: the only 'civilization' he denounces is that responsible for the atom bomb and the mind-numbing repetitions of television.

Although *The Dharma Bums* was conceived as a kind of sequel to *On the Road*, Kerouac's use of more traditional sentence structures, his distaste for popular culture (television) and his citations of Pound, Whitman and Shakespeare mark a stylistic shift. The shorter sentences (than those of *The Subterraneans* or *Visions of Cody*, for example) show the trace of Gary Snyder's influence in their fusion of West and East in traditional syntax coupled with the attempt to imitate haiku by – as Kerouac wrote in his introduction to his *Scattered Poems* – 'pointing out things directly, purely, concretely, no abstractions or explanations, wham wham the true blue song of man'.[47] In addition, Kerouac inserts actual haiku within the narrative, including Shiki's 'The Sparrow hops along the veranda, with wet feet' and those that Ray and Japhy make up, as well as

[47] Jack Kerouac, 'The Origins of Joy in Poetry', introduction to *Scattered Poems* (San Francisco: City Lights, 1985).

composing haiku-like sentences such as 'we all got dizzy and drunk. It was a wild night' and 'He bought an aluminium pot holder and made me a gift of it.'[48]

In the final pages of the novel, Ray takes Japhy's advice and accepts a job as fire lookout on Desolation Peak (as did Kerouac himself), where he experiences two months of enforced solitude. He claims that the experience reveals that Japhy had been right and that he feels 'really free'. With nothing to do but report on any fires, Ray is able to regress to a life with virtually no responsibilities, and notes that 'my hair was long, my eyes blue in the mirror, my skin tanned and happy'. When he leaves the mountain, he adds 'Blah!' to his departing prayer, 'because I knew that shack and that mountain would understand what that meant', in an attestation of his unity with nature.[49] Gerald Nicosia has interpreted the comment as meaning 'that wisdom is unspeakable, that the value of life cannot be inventoried but only lived'. For Nicosia, 'That insight was as desperately needed amid the Madison Avenue hype of the Fifties as it was painful for America's conspicuous consumers to practice.'[50]

Earlier, however, Nicosia suggests that 'the chief change wrought on Desolation was that [Kerouac] no longer balked at lying to himself'.[51] A comparison with *Desolation Angels*, in which Kerouac records his time as a lookout in much more detail, reveals how much of the boredom and loneliness of solitude Kerouac omitted from *The Dharma Bums*. Although the change is clearly predicated on the need to give the novel a structural wholeness, with Ray learning what Japhy has preached, the short space allocated to the description of such a

---

[48] Kerouac, *The Dharma Bums*, pp. 46, 77, 79.
[49] Ibid., pp. 172, 173.
[50] Nicosia, *Memory Babe*, p. 563.
[51] Ibid., p. 528.

long period of isolation does not convey the emotional extremes of Ray's seclusion convincingly. Ultimately, *The Dharma Bums* lacks the self-examination of, for example, *The Subterraneans*, and the effect is to strip a novel whose subject matter is the limits of the western ethos of the angst that would be expected of a part of 'The Legend of Duluoz'. In contrast, in *Big Sur* – the novel that effectively marks the end of Kerouac's time as a Beat – the 'Legend' represents the painful effects of fame, the city and solitude on his consciousness.

Among the Beat Generation, 3: *Big Sur*

Big Sur is both a return to and departure from the earlier volumes in 'The Legend of Duluoz'. On the one hand, it marks a return to the spontaneous prose of Kerouac's most creative period (1952–3), during which he had written six of his most impressive novels; on the other, it is a book in which Duluoz becomes the centre of attention, as opposed to the passive partner who 'shambled after . . . people who interested me'[52] in *On the Road* and *The Dharma Bums*. The experiences related in the book link the themes of the 'Legend' in its entirety and compel Kerouac to admit that his visions of both himself and of America are myths that conceal darker truths.

Barry Gifford has observed that

> When *Big Sur* was published . . . it received excellent reviews perhaps because it portrayed the 'King of the Beats' brought low, perhaps because of its frightening honesty. The book, unlike those which had been published before, portrayed Duluoz as a man who could feel as well as observe.[53]

---

[52] Kerouac, *On the Road*, p. 11.
[53] Lee, *Jack's Book*, p. 295.

There is no doubt that by the early 1960s Kerouac was experiencing a sharp physical and emotional decline, largely as a result of chronic alcoholism that was exacerbated by his inability to cope with the fame stemming from the success of *On the Road*. As he explains at the start of *Big Sur*, he feels hounded by young admirers, with the result that he has been 'drunk practically all the time' and feels that he is 'surrounded and outnumbered and [has] to get away again to solitude or die'.[54] In addition, with the emergence of both the 'beatnik' phenomenon and of the Greenwich Village folk music revival, there was a strong sense that many young Americans were wearying of a culture of consumption that they perceived as inauthentic and exploitative, and, in this context, Gifford is probably correct to suggest that many of the more conservative critics were delighted to see Kerouac receive what was, in their view, a deserved comeuppance.

Being famous makes Duluoz face the impossibility of realizing Ray Smith's dream of 'doing anything I wanted',[55] a goal that – within the parameters of their own ideologies – resided at the heart of Beat ambition. Ironically, of course, it is Kerouac's status as so-called leader of the Beat Generation that thrusts responsibility upon the privacy-seeking author:

> I've been driven mad for three years by endless telegrams, phonecalls, requests, mail, visitors, reporters, snoopers (a big voice saying in my basement window as I prepare to write a story: ARE YOU BUSY?) or the time the reporter ran upstairs to my bedroom as I sat there in my pyjamas trying to write down a dream – Teenagers jumping the six-foot fence I'd had built around my yard for privacy – Parties with bottles yelling at my study window 'Come on out and get drunk, all work and

---

[54] Kerouac, *Big Sur*, p. 8.
[55] Kerouac, *The Dharma Bums*, p. 107.

no play makes Jack a dull boy!' – A woman coming to my door and saying 'I'm not going to ask you if you're Jack Duluoz because I know he wears a beard, can you tell me where I can find him, I want a real beatnik at my annual Shindig party' – Drunken visitors puking in my study, stealing books and even pencils . . . all over America highschool and college kids thinking 'Jack Duluoz is twenty-six years old and on the road all the time hitch hiking' while there I was almost forty years old, bored and jaded in a roomette bunk crashin across that Salt Flat.[56]

Kerouac outlines the realities, as opposed to his earlier fantasies, of the American Dream. As a result of the publicity surrounding his work, the world that he described in his earlier novels had been transformed into the latest vehicle for teenage fashion, in a trivializing process that bore no relation to Kerouac's own message. Like Neal Cassady, who had been arrested by an undercover policeman and jailed on drug charges largely because of his celebrity as 'Dean Moriarty', Kerouac was forced to confront the unintended consequences of the success of *On the Road*. While Kerouac/Duluoz is – as the 'Legend' makes clear – essentially a conservative character, his own words are no match for the sensationalizing efforts of the popular media and the audience of school and college kids eager to swallow their message.

The effects of fame on Kerouac and of the feeling that his message had been misunderstood are described succinctly by Joyce Johnson in her memoir *Minor Characters* (1983). Although the book's focus is on the women who tend to occupy the margins of Kerouac's 1950s world, it also contains recollections of the days following the publication of *On the Road*. Kerouac's life – and that of other Beats – was transformed by Gilbert

---

[56] Kerouac, *Big Sur*, pp. 8–9.

Millstein's ecstatic *New York Times* review of *Road* which turned the by then thirty-five-year-old author into the latest overnight sensation. Recollecting how Kerouac's patient explanations of the meaning of 'Beat' were ignored by journalists eager to articulate their own preconceptions, Johnson (who, as Joyce Glassman, had been Kerouac's girlfriend when *On the Road* was published) points out that

> No one had much patience for derivations by 1957. People wanted the quick thing, language reduced to slogans, ideas flashed like advertisements, never quite sinking in before the next one came along. 'Beat Generation' sold books, sold black turtleneck sweaters and bongos, berets and dark glasses, sold a way of life that seemed like dangerous fun – thus to be either condemned or imitated. Suburban couples could have beatnik parties on Saturday nights and drink too much and fondle each other's wives . . . 'Beat Generation' had implied history, some process of development. But with the right accessories, 'beatniks' could be created on the spot.[57]

When 'The Legend of Duluoz' is read in its entirety, there is poignant irony in the devastating effect that publicity had on Kerouac. In *The Subterraneans*, Kerouac's skilful improvisations on jazz and African American speech appeared to be at odds with his flawed attitudes to race; in *Big Sur*, the return to a similar style corresponds with his (and Duluoz's) own tormented spirit. Although it would, of course, be misguided to suggest that Duluoz's role as a notorious author subjects him to the humiliations suffered by ethnic minorities in the United States at the time, it does impose similar restrictions on personal freedom. In the same way that Leo Percepied expected certain actions from Mardou or from Charlie Parker, Duluoz is now the victim of

[57] Joyce Johnson, *Minor Characters*, extract in *The Portable Beat Reader*, edited by Anne Charters (New York: Penguin, 1992), p. 480.

other people's preconceptions, and nothing he can do will alter their convictions.

In a more or less direct transposition of Kerouac's own actions, Duluoz's response to his celebrity is to head west (again) and to seek solitude in a cabin next to the Pacific Ocean. *On the Road* and even *The Dharma Bums* (staged almost a decade later) represent an ongoing innocence about the west, even if that innocence is threatened by the encroachment of modernity, but Duluoz's return to California suggests that the standardization of the nation is now complete. On his first morning at Monsanto's cabin, he awakes to see the wreck of a car 'like a terrifying poem about America one could write':

> The automobile that crashed through the bridge rail a decade
> ago and fell 1000 feet straight down and landed upside down,
> is still there now, an upsidedown chassis of rust in a strewn
> skitter of sea-eaten tires, old spokes, old car seats sprung with
> straw, one sad fuel pump and no more people.[58]

Ever the quintessential Beat philosopher, Duluoz sees the wreck as a metaphor for the dangerous forces unleashed by technology. The A-bomb means the possibility of the destruction of the human race, with rusting metal the only reminder of what had once existed. As John Tytell has noted, Duluoz's return makes him realize that the west of his dreams has now become a 'tentacled megapolis'.[59] Whereas San Francisco had always represented the frontier for Kerouac, as in *The Dharma Bums* or 'October in the Railroad Earth', in *Big Sur* that frontier has been overrun and the old heroes 'have been hemmed in and surrounded and outnumbered – The circle's closed on the old heroes of the night.'[60]

[58] Ibid., pp. 19, 16.
[59] Tytell, *Naked Angels*, p. 207.
[60] Kerouac, *Big Sur*, p. 61.

In a way, however, the wrecked automobile symbolizes something more personal, the collapse of Kerouac's own dream of Beat Generation freedom as realized in the transcontinental drives with Dean that are the subject of some of the most joyous passages in *On the Road*. *Big Sur* is the moment when Kerouac finally admits to the hollowness of his own dreams, with the implication that he has been duped all along – the gullible immigrant who believed what he had been told about the nation. Whereas in the early volumes of the 'Legend', Kerouac incorporated mass-cultural devices as a way to shape his own material, in *Big Sur* he self-consciously rejects them, cutting through the 'big designed mankind cartoon of a man standing facing the rising sun with strong shoulders with a plough at his feet' to reveal the 'necktied governor' manipulating the illusion. At last (perhaps acknowledging the inescapability of popular cultural referents and drawing upon another echo from *The Wizard of Oz*), he admits that the America he had once cherished is a fraud.

Big Sur suggests that Kerouac identifies his own complicity in the culture industry that he has come to despise. Whereas, in *The Dharma Bums*, Ray Smith claims that his period of solitude on Desolation Peak brings rejuvenation and a renewed bond with Nature, Duluoz's spell in Monsanto's cabin appears to mark a rejection by Nature. He believes that his visit will give him 'peace' and the chance to 'Go back to childhood, just eat apples and read [his] Catechism – sit on curbstones, the hell with the hot lights of Hollywood.' Quoting Emerson's assertion that 'Life is not an apology,' Duluoz tries to convince himself that 'once again I'm Ti Jean the child'. The early days of his time at the cabin represent a life of simple pleasures, in which he attempts to recreate and celebrate Emerson, Thoreau and Whitman's vision of America. And yet, by the fourth day, he wonders whether he is 'Already bored?' and starts to long for cities that he knows will be 'sickening'. The longing for company is equated with a recognition of an unbridgeable gap between Man and Nature, feeling that the sea 'didn't want me there . . . the sea has its waves, the man has his fireside, period'.[61]

Although these incidents foreshadow what follows, they do not fully prepare the reader for the harrowing account of Duluoz's breakdown that occupies the concluding chapters of *Big Sur*. Having spent much of the 'Legend' observing the actions of others, Kerouac produces some of his finest – and most controlled – prose in his description of the devastating and uncontrollable effects of the delirium tremens that afflicts Duluoz:

> If I try to close my eyes some elastic pulls them open again – if I try to turn over the whole universe turns over with me but it's no better on the other side of the universe – I realize I may never come out of this and my mother is waiting for me at home praying for me because she must know what's happening tonight, I cry out to her to pray and help me – I remember my cat for the first time in three hours and let out a yell that scares Billie – . . . and I can't help thinking she and Dave and Romana are all secretly awake waiting for me to die – 'For what reason?' I'm thinking 'this secret poisoning society, I know, it's because I'm a Catholic, it's a big anti-Catholic scheme, it's Communists destroying everything . . . I always thought Romana was a Communist being a Rumanian . . .' But soon my thoughts aren't even as 'rational' as that any more but become hours of raving – I keep waving at my ears – I'm afraid to close my eyes for all the turmoiled universes I see tilting and expanding suddenly exploding suddenly clawing in to my center, faces, yelling mouths, long haired yellers, sudden evil confidences, sudden rat-tat-tats of cerebral committees arguing about 'Jack' and talking about him as if he wasnt there – Aimless moments when

---

[61]   Ibid., pp. 20, 30, 73, 39.

I'm waiting for more voices and suddenly the wind explodes huge groans in the million treetop leaves that sound like the moon gone mad.[62]

Within a single sentence (interrupted by dashes at the start, but gaining momentum towards the staccato succession of 'sudden' tortures), Kerouac confesses to all the paranoia and prejudice that surface throughout his work. In time of need, he immediately and instinctively turns to his mother and suspects the motives of his friends. Both his fear of alienation from the 'mainstream' and his hatred of any threat to America emerge in his anxieties about being a Catholic and in his indoctrinated anti-communist sentiments. With his rejection by an actively hostile natural world, Duluoz's thoughts turn inward, but find no relief in the reminders of what took him to Big Sur in the first place.

The source of Duluoz's salvation is an ironic epitaph to his experiments with Eastern religion in *The Dharma Bums* and *Big Sur*. In fulfilment of Japhy Ryder's prophecy ('I can just see you on your deathbed kissing the cross like some old Karamazov'), Duluoz has a vision of the Cross and exclaims, 'I just let myself go into death and the Cross: as soon as that happens I slowly sink back into life . . . and I say through all the noise of the voices, "I'm with you, Jesus, for always, thank you." '[63] Although his 'horrors' continue, the moment prepares Duluoz for his return to his mother's house. His admission that he needs Jesus is, as Ann Charters suggests, 'the ultimate evidence of his lack of self-reliance . . . the opposite of what Emerson had in mind in his essays'[64] and the opposite of Kerouac's Beat vision. In *Doctor Sax*, Duluoz recalls how, when he ran away from home at age eight,

---

[62] Ibid., pp. 170–1.
[63] Ibid., p. 172.
[64] Anne Charters, *Kerouac* (San Francisco: Straight Arrow, 1973), p. 334.

he 'judged I was being torn from my mother's womb with each step from Home Lowell into the Unknown'.[65] Thirty years later, the only way to ease his pain is to return to his childhood dependency on Mémère and the Church. Never again did Kerouac leave home for more than a month.

Although Kerouac continued to write until his death in 1969, *Big Sur* marks the chronological end of 'The Legend of Duluoz'. *Satori in Paris* relates his ten-day trip to France in 1965, but is no more than what John Tytell calls an 'anecdotal sketch' about Kerouac's attempts to 'discover the genealogy of the Kerouac name'.[66] As Charters has observed, the events recounted in *Big Sur* 'marked the turning point into his later years. His breakdown at the cabin sealed him off from the vitality and affirmations of his earlier life and his earlier books. He kept on, but the force was gone, and his life was shadowed and aimless.'[67] Settled with his mother and, later, his third wife (whom Kerouac's daughter, Jan, termed 'another mother to take care of them both' – that is, Kerouac and the now infirm Mémère[68]), all Kerouac could do was relive his past in *Vanity of Duluoz*, a novel that revisits the years before his first journey west. Although it is one of Kerouac's finest novels, it offers no suggestion that he had anything else to look forward to: the book is dedicated to 'Stavroula' (the name of his third wife), which, in Greek, means 'From the Cross'.

[65] Kerouac, *Doctor Sax*, p. 99.
[66] Tytell, *Naked Angels*, p. 208.
[67] Charters, *Kerouac*, p. 340.
[68] Jan Kerouac, *Baby Driver* (1981), extract in *The Portable Beat Reader*, p. 493.

5

Other voices

The period between the end of the Second World War and the election of John F. Kennedy is often – as I have suggested earlier in this book – seen as an age of conformity, in which material prosperity offset the fears and threats posed by the Cold War, and in which the majority of Americans led contented suburban lives. This picture is, of course, far from complete and innumerable analysts have proposed that even in the heartlands of mainstream America discontent was rife. Although a sociologist such as Paul Goodman could remain generally unsympathetic to the Beat remedies to middle-class American life, his best-known book *Growing up Absurd* (1960) suggests that the alienation expressed so passionately in Allen Ginsberg's 'Howl' pervaded American society. For Goodman, 'real opportunities for worthwhile experience'[1] are almost entirely absent in a society where men are allocated to jobs wherever they are required in the productive system, and persuaded to consume worthless goods through incessant advertising and peer pressure. Likewise, Betty Friedan's *The Feminine Mystique* (1963) investigates discontent in the world of the American housewife, yet discovers a sense of alienation remarkably similar to that expressed by the Beat Generation.

For both Goodman and Friedan, one of the principal problems for Americans in the 1950s was finding means to express their unhappiness. For Friedan, the sheer weight of expertise utilized in telling women how wonderful their lives

[1] Paul Goodman, *Growing up Absurd: Problems of Youth in the Organized Society* (New York: Vintage Books, 1960), p. 12.

were made it almost impossible to articulate 'The Problem that Has No Name'. For Goodman, the solution lies in a return to the past and his critique stems from a perspective based closely upon the earlier 'inner-directed' model of American selfhood, in which personal fulfilment comes from meaningful, satisfying employment, rather than from consumption. As such, he rejects the twentieth-century replacement of production-based capitalism with the culture of consumption and manifests nostalgia for an earlier American society with values based in 'true' culture.

The sense of widespread – and often hidden or unarticulated – alienation felt by many Americans during the period examined by Goodman and Friedan (the second half of the 1950s) helps one to understand the transformation of the Beats from a small group of artists working mainly in New York and San Francisco and reaching out to a small audience into a fully fledged 'Generation' that put *On the Road* in the bestseller list and saw 'Howl' as the articulation of their discontents. One result of this change was the transformation of 'Beat' to 'beatnik' – a process through which the 'cool' persona became the latest commodification to be marketed by a fashion industry discovering the economic potential of the teen and twenty-something market, and in which no fashionable party was complete without the presence of a 'rent-a-beatnik' figure chanting meaningless poetry and lightweight catchphrases.

But this should not lead us to see the expanding appeal of the Beat Generation at this time as an entirely negative manifestation of corporate capitalism's ability to appropriate a subculture, drain it of its counter-hegemonic zeal and re-brand it as 'lifestyle' chic. During the 1950s, a whole new wave of Beat writers emerged, many born in the early 1930s and thus a decade or more younger than Kerouac and Burroughs and several years younger than Ginsberg and Cassady. Some – such as Michael McClure and Gregory Corso – swiftly became integral members of the core Beat community, but others either worked in other

BEATNIKS

The success of *On the Road* and the heightened profile that this brought to writers who had spent a decade or more struggling even to find publishers for their work inevitably resulted in a backlash from conservative critics anxious to protect their own version of American culture and label anything that challenged this deviant or un-American. While the Beat Generation went to great lengths to explain the spirituality at the heart of their work and the sincerity of their vision, the media were generally more interested in lampooning a community that they character-ized as lazy, inarticulate and quite possibly a threat to national stability. This mood reflected a culture in which almost any activity that deviated from the norms of American life, as repre-sented on television and in popular lifestyle magazines, would swiftly be identified as part of a wider communist conspiracy to undermine American values. Indeed, at the 1960 Republican Convention, FBI boss J. Edgar Hoover listed 'communists, eggheads and beatniks' as the three gravest challenges confronting the nation.

Hoover's reference to 'beatniks' drew on a term first used by Herb Caen in an article in the *San Francisco Chronicle* in April 1958. *Sputnik 1*, the first man-made object to orbit the earth, had been launched by the Soviet Union the previous October, and its success provoked a major crisis in the American political and scientific communities that had complacently assumed that the United States was well ahead in the space race. The response ultimately led to the *Apollo* moon landings that commenced in 1969, but also involved the establishment of NASA, major financial investment in the training of a new generation of American engineers and significant increases in support for other scientific projects.

Caen's conflation of Beat and *Sputnik* had the obvious effect of linking the Beat Generation with Cold War enemies and encour-aged an older generation to be suspicious of a movement that sought to subvert their teenage children. Ironically, however, the

BEATNIKS (*cont.*)

beatnik soon came to occupy a range of other positions in popular culture. Caen's idea that the beatnik was an idler was rapidly picked up elsewhere: the caricature of bongo-playing, goatee-bearded men in berets and hooped T-shirts or turtleneck sweaters became a mainstay of cartoonists, while the quintessential work-shy beatnik Maynard G. Krebs (played by Bob Denver) was integral to the success of the television sitcom *The Many Loves of Dobie Gillis* (1959–63) and probably shaped many Americans' impressions of Beat life.

At another extreme, the beatnik caricature could be presented as a violent criminal, willing to use a knife or gun to satisfy his psychopathic urges. While this type had initially been proposed by Norman Mailer, in his essay 'The White Negro' (1957), low-budget and sensationalist Hollywood movies such as *The Beat Generation* (1959) and *The Beatniks* (1960) stripped away the complexities of Mailer's thesis of existential angst and portrayed beatniks as little more than unthinking criminal thugs.

But while the beatnik could serve as public enemy number one, *he* – and his long-haired, 'cool' girlfriend, always dressed in black – could also represent a marketing opportunity for corporations increasingly aware of the youth market.

While Beat ideology recognized individual differences and encouraged everyone to reject conformity and develop their own identity and artistic style, the beatnik was a caricature stripped bare of personal idiosyncrasies. A positive consequence of this was that many young people initially attracted by the latest look – in which 'Beat' clothes became the latest fashion – did subsequently turn to and appreciate the literature that had prompted the commercial response. Nevertheless, the principal legacy of the 'beatnik phenomenon' was negative, and ensured that most Americans remained ignorant of the true ideals of Beat practitioners such as Kerouac and Ginsberg.

geographical regions, remained relatively unknown or sought acceptance elsewhere because, as women or non-white artists, they tended to remain largely unseen within a movement characterized as white and male. While – as the previous chapter explains – the Beat Generation (as imagined by Ginsberg, Kerouac and others) was adept at promoting homosocial (and often homosexual) voices, the construction of a Beat canon has tended to marginalize women and non-white writers. In part, this is a direct result of Ginsberg's pivotal role in championing his friends and close acquaintances; in part, it is the product of a literary establishment that, until long after the heyday of the Beat Generation, focused its attentions overwhelmingly on white male authors. Nevertheless, as photographs and memoirs make clear, the Beat community was multi-ethnic and included many women writers.

Rather than listing numerous examples of representatives of those groups 'unfairly' excluded from dominant histories, this chapter of the *Beginner's Guide* will focus on a selection of writers – notably Joyce Johnson, Hettie Jones, Diane di Prima, LeRoi Jones/Amiri Baraka and Carolyn Cassady – whose work challenges stereotypical memories of Beat. I will focus not only on how these writers contributed to Beat culture and writing, but also on how they underwent processes of reinvention in their efforts to express their ideas in ways that were not always possible within the narrative shaped by the popularity and pivotal positions of Kerouac and Ginsberg. Di Prima's determination to succeed as a writer on her own terms, independent of male patronage, Cassady's re-imagining of her position in the triangular relationship she shared with Kerouac and Neal Cassady, and Jones's move from Beat to Black Arts will be used to examine the internal politics of Beat culture.

Writing off the road: Joyce Johnson, Hettie Jones, Diane di Prima and Carolyn Cassady

When the *New York Times* published the review of *On the Road* by Gilbert Millstein that would transform the lives of the Beat Generation, Kerouac was staying with his then girlfriend Joyce Glassman (later Joyce Johnson, b. 1935) in her New York apartment. In one of the moments of Beat history that have become immortalized through retelling, Kerouac and Joyce took a late-night walk down to the news-stand at 66th Street and Broadway and picked up a copy of the following day's paper, which contained the review announcing the 'historic occasion' of the publication of the 'most beautifully executed, the clearest and the most important utterance yet made by the generation Kerouac himself named years ago as "beat", and whose principal avatar he is'.[2] While the review was more positive than anyone could possibly have hoped, it also had disastrous repercussions for Kerouac, who found fame hard to deal with after so many years of obscurity. The procession of reporters and fans that materialized at Glassman's door in the following days arrived expecting to find a Moriartyesque character and the naturally shy (and by now thirty-five years old) Kerouac responded by indulging in one of his increasingly frequent drinking binges – although these were now as likely to involve the consumption of expensive Scotch as cheap wine.

The catastrophic effects of fame on Kerouac have been written about extensively. What is less well known is the manner in which his success had significant ramifications for others within his circle. Glassman had met Kerouac on a blind date set up by Allen Ginsberg in January 1957 and – although

---

[2] Gilbert Millstein, review of *On the Road*, *New York Times*, 5 September 1957.

the relationship was stalled by Kerouac's trip to visit William Burroughs in Tangier, where Burroughs was typing up sections of *Naked Lunch*, and by Kerouac's ill-conceived and short-lived plans to move with Mémêre to California – they were involved in a serious relationship, albeit one that Glassman realized was sure to be short-lived. Like Joan Vollmer and Edie Parker, Glassman had studied at Barnard College, although – aged twenty-one when she met Kerouac in 1957 – she was much younger. Nevertheless, she was already an aspiring writer with a contract and advance for her debut novel, *Come and Join the Dance* (1962), as well as being an independent spirit who had swapped the comforts of a wealthy middle-class home for the precarious excitement of life in Greenwich Village.

Glassman's life and career epitomize the difficulties confronted by female Beats. First, as a woman, it was impossible for her to undertake the kinds of trip made by Kerouac, since hitch-hiking or hopping freights would be far too dangerous. Thus, like other writers including Diane di Prima, she remained in New York while the male Beats roamed America and the wider world. But the difficulties were not solely those of lifestyle: as Joyce Johnson, Glassman is best known for her memoir, *Minor Characters* (1983), in which she chronicles the lives of the women involved in the Beat scene as well as their relationships with the pivotal male figures. The book highlights both the dependency on women exhibited by Kerouac and other male Beats and the damaging consequences for the women who were seen as subservient despite their own talents and aspirations.

Come and Join the Dance is in many ways a more interesting text, but is now – along with her other novels – out of print. In it, Susan Leavitt, a thinly disguised version of Glassman, experiences a sexual awakening as she breaks away from the rigid life mapped out for her by her parents, meets a selection of 'Beat' characters and elects to fail her college course in New York

City. In summary, it sounds like a familiar Beat narrative, but this disguises the extent to which Glassman differs from an author like Kerouac and hints at a greater diversity of Beat practice than is commonly assumed when the Kerouac–Ginsberg mantra of 'first thought, best thought' is taken to represent the compositional processes of *all* Beats. Glassman has always been happy to acknowledge the importance of a lengthy process of revision in her writing and is also probably more attuned to the crafted prose of Henry James and Virginia Woolf than to the rougher models such as Herman Melville and Jack London cited by Kerouac.

Glassman's relationship with Kerouac was clearly a mixed blessing: while it did place her in a privileged position in Beat history, it has also shaped critical and commercial responses to her own work. There always seems to be an audience for her reminiscences about Kerouac, but it has been hard for her to sustain a career as an author distanced from that world. The impression of the Beat Generation as a club for men seeking freedom in travel, sex and jazz is not exactly a distortion, given that the figures perceived as coining its name and shaping its destiny were the small group of men who remain its most famous practitioners, but it is not quite the whole picture either. A writer like Joyce Glassman reminds us of the wider social circle within which Kerouac, Ginsberg, Burroughs and Corso functioned, and the different perspectives offered by the writing of someone who – as a woman – was by definition excluded from the homosocial hub of the movement are useful in under-standing the consequences for others that stemmed from the men's quest for freedom.

Like Glassman, Hettie Jones tends to be remembered more for her relationship with a male author rather than for her own achievements. Born in Brooklyn in 1934 into a wealthy Jewish family and brought up in Laurelton, Queens, Hettie Cohen spent her adolescence in ways similar to those of many of the artists discussed in this book. Fond of reading and of jazz, and with aspirations to be a writer, she had the usual round of fallings out with her family and frequenting jazz clubs and coffee houses. Her life changed dramatically when she met – and subsequently married – LeRoi Jones, an ambitious young African American poet.

LEROI JONES/AMIRI BARAKA

While prominent poets such as Allen Ginsberg were happy to promote and celebrate the Beat Generation's values and works long after its moment at the heart of countercultural American life had passed, other figures were keen to distance themselves from its legacy. LeRoi Jones (later Amiri Baraka; b. 1934) has spent his life as an artist and political activist, at times drawing upon the lessons he learned in Greenwich Village in the 1950s and early 1960s, but his rejection of his Beat colleagues and move away from the Village are indicative of the sense – shared by other African American writers such as James Baldwin – that the Beat Generation's embrace of the 'Negro' was far from equivocal.

Jones was born in Newark in 1934 and raised in a family that he himself described as part of the emergent black bourgeoisie. Following periods of study at Rutgers, Columbia and Howard Universities (and without obtaining a degree), he served in the US Air Force until he was given a dishonourable discharge for being suspected of communist sympathies. He then spent several years in the Greenwich Village Beat scene, writing poetry, editing *Yugen* magazine, founding Totem Press and marrying fellow Beat the Jewish (and white) Hettie Cohen. Like many other Beats, Jones developed an interest in jazz, but – unlike his white counterparts – he refined this interest as a way of scrutinizing the position of the African American in United States society. From 1960, when he visited Cuba, he adopted an increasingly militant position on race, leading to inevitable tensions within the largely white Village scene. These tensions culminated in his decision to leave his wife

LEROI JONES/AMIRI BARAKA (*cont.*)

and children and abandon the Village, to live first in Harlem and later – after a short spell in San Francisco – in Newark. The final separation seems largely to have been prompted by the killing of Malcolm X, although Jones's marriage had been strained for some time before this.

Jones was pivotal in the establishment of the Black Arts Movement in the 1960s, initiating a poetry that called for cultural revolution and the rise of Black Power. He was a staunch supporter of Kenneth Gibson during Gibson's (successful) campaign to become the first non-white mayor of Newark and – although his interest has turned increasingly to the global politics of anti-imperialist movements – has continued to be a vocal critic of the state's attitudes to African Americans.

Jones/Baraka's writings give a solid impression of his ideology at different stages of his career, and mark his move away from Beat culture. Early poems such as 'In Memory of Radio' and 'Way out West' (1961) namecheck fellow Beats Kerouac and Gary Snyder, and echo many of their values, including nostalgia for the popular culture of their childhoods. This generally positive assess-ment of Greenwich Village as a multiracial community with the potential to challenge the racism at the core of dominant American culture is developed more fully in *Blues People* (1963), one of the most significant studies of jazz ever to have been published. Jones goes to great length to explain the similarities between the positions of young urban African Americans and alienated Beats (and like-minded artists such as Jackson Pollock), and points out that the overlaps between jazz, Beat Generation poetry and prose and Abstract Expressionist painting provoked a hostile – and entirely predictable – response from the traditionalist critics who controlled the mass media. His position on the inter-racial dimensions of artistic exchange is also almost entirely positive, the 'cross-fertilization' between jazz and white arts offer-ing a model of lateral integration in which the arts and values of minority cultures are accepted by the dominant one and used to

LEROI JONES/AMIRI BARAKA (*cont.*)

enrich the life of both communities. He contrasts this model with the more familiar 'melting pot' ideology that had conditioned immigrants and African Americans to consider their own cultures to be inferior to an American ideal to which they should all aspire.

This near-utopian reading of the potential of Greenwich Village (Beat Generation) life to reshape national ideas about race was, however, short-lived, in part because Jones felt that a chasm existed between the words of fellow Beats and their residual attitudes towards race. Only a year after the publication of *Blues People*, poems including 'Black Dada Nihilismus' (1964) not only questioned the viability of multiracial cohabitation, but also imagine a disturbing split with white America, including the racially mixed Beat culture of lower Manhattan. The bohemian artistic community of the early 1960s was still small and Jones's rejection of it in such provocative and violent terms would have been hard to overlook for figures such as Allen Ginsberg, who regarded Jones as an integral member of the 'black white hip' community. Ironically, however, the split led directly to commercial and critical success. In 1964, Jones's play *Dutchman*, in which a naive black college student is tormented and ultimately murdered by an abusive white woman in a subway car that symbolizes a deeply troubled national racial unconscious, won the Obie Award for best off-Broadway play and brought him a raised profile in the American artistic community.

The distance that Baraka has travelled since his days in Greenwich Village bohemia can also be charted by his readiness to include anti-Semitic views in his poetry and essays. In the 1960s, these works propagated views expressed by the Nation of Islam – a radical Black Power group demanding the right to establish their own state in America or elsewhere and hostile to white and Jewish Americans – but Baraka subsequently adopted a more conventional Marxist perspective in his attacks on the state. While the work of fellow Beats such as Kerouac, Ginsberg and even Burroughs has been accommodated within American popular

LEROI JONES/AMIRI BARAKA (*cont.*)

culture, and is regularly referenced in television commercials and mainstream shows, Baraka has become, if anything, an even more controversial figure in the twenty-first century. In particular, his post-9/11 poem, 'Somebody Blew up America', in which he chronicles the abuses perpetrated across time in the name of 'American' values and suggests that Israeli workers knew in advance what would occur and stayed clear of the Twin Towers on 11 September 2001, provoked a media frenzy and led to Baraka's position as Poet Laureate of New Jersey being terminated and to him becoming persona non grata on many campuses throughout the United States.

Although Jones also came from a respectable middle-class home, it is unsurprising that Hettie's parents disapproved strenuously of the match. Even in the Bohemian atmosphere of Greenwich Village, a mixed-race marriage was unusual, but LeRoi and Hettie established themselves at the heart of the Beat scene both through their joint editorship of *Yugen*, a literary journal that published works by most of the leading Beat writers, and as hosts of the hippest parties in town. They also set up Totem Press, an independent organization dedicated to publishing and promoting work by emerging young artists, often with a political agenda that would preclude their acceptance by more mainstream publishers. Nevertheless, it was evident to everyone that LeRoi was the writer destined for stardom and Hettie's own poems made little impression.

Jones tells her life story in *How I Became Hettie Jones* (1990), one of the most significant autobiographies to be produced by someone living in the midst of the Beat Generation. Not only does the book contain her impressions of figures such as Ginsberg and Kerouac, and a lengthy account of her friendship with Joyce Glassman; it also analyses the multiple instances of marginalization that she experienced as a Beat, a woman, and a Jew married to an African American in a culture not always welcoming to any one of these categories. *How I Became Hettie Jones* also offers insights on the reasons for the collapse of the Beat Generation, in particular in its telling of LeRoi Jones's transformation into Amiri Baraka, the left-wing Black Nationalist who abandoned his white wife (*because* she was white) and left the Village scene in which he had made his name in order to pursue a radical racial agenda in Newark.

In some ways, Hettie Jones's lifestyle was not entirely unconventional. While her relationship with a black man and role in the underground press were signs of her radicalism, her practical skills in raising two daughters on a tight budget while her womanizing husband spent increasing periods of time away from home are not atypical of the experiences of many American women. In contrast, Diane di Prima (b. 1934) – in addition to having a child with LeRoi Jones – is perhaps the supreme example of a Beat woman able not only to challenge the norms of American life through her participation in the Beat Generation but also to match the male Beats as a successful writer with a unique voice.

While many of the Beat Generation came from middle-class families with comfortable incomes, di Prima grew up in a working-class Italian American community in Brooklyn. Like Jack Kerouac's parents – French Canadian immigrants who had moved to New England – and many other ethnic migrants during the opening decades of the twentieth century, di Prima's family accepted the promises of the American Dream implicitly and expected their children to be better educated than they had been and to move into well-paid professional jobs that would provide them with a comfortable lifestyle. Like Kerouac, di Prima turned away from this narrative, dropping out of Swarthmore College and moving into a rat-infested cold-water flat in the tenements that were later demolished to make way for the Lincoln Center. As her autobiography, *Recollections of My Life as a Woman* (2001), makes clear, Di Prima has always been aware that this kind of rejection of convention has more serious ramifications for women than it does for men. Looking back at her move to Manhattan, she notes,

> What I do know is that choosing to be an artist: writer, dancer, painter, musician, actor, photographer, sculptor, you name it, choosing to be any of these things in the world I grew up in, the world of the 40s and early 50s, was choosing as completely as possible for those times the life of the renunciant. Life of the wandering sadhu, itinerant saint, outside the confines and laws of that particular and peculiar culture.[3]

At college, di Prima established a close group of female friends, but her prose writing – both *Recollections* and her fictionalized autobiography, *Memoirs of a Beatnik* (1969) – illustrates the different forms of suffering that they experienced as young women who dared to challenge conventional values in the 1950s. In *Memoirs of a Beatnik*, for example, one friend (Tomi) is unable to move to Greenwich Village because she feels that she cannot abandon her mother to a life alone in their severely dysfunctional family. Di Prima's point is that the young male Beats were generally spared the extreme forms of emotional manipulation that young women's families would apply in reminding their offspring of familial responsibilities incompatible with the freedoms promised by Beat life.

These things make di Prima's subsequent triumphs all the more commendable. Professionally, she was responsible – alongside LeRoi Jones – for *The Floating Bear*, a monthly magazine that published their own writings alongside work by Kerouac,

---

[3] Diane di Prima, *Recollections of My Life as a Woman: The New York Years* (New York: Viking Penguin, 2001), p. 101.

Burroughs and many other well- and lesser-known Beats. In addition, her debut collection of poetry, *This Kind of Bird Flies Backward* (1958), was a critically acclaimed book that is a very rare example of a work by a woman that received high praise from Allen Ginsberg. Di Prima has enjoyed a half-century-long career marked by significant highs, including receiving major grants and being shortlisted for the position of Poet Laureate of California. Of equal significance, however, is the degree to which she has been able constantly to re-invent herself in a challenge to male efforts to classify her as a 'Beat chick' or hippie earth mother. *Memoirs of a Beatnik* (a curious hybrid of pornographic potboiler and straight autobiography) chronicles the years leading to the publication of *This Kind of Bird Flies Backward* and the birth of di Prima's first child. It represents di Prima as being able to manipulate a fluid sense of self that is defined as an ongoing process of re-invention able to outwit male efforts to categorize her. The book concludes with di Prima electing to become a single mother – a challenge not only to dominant images of suburban married bliss, but also to leading male Beats, such as Kerouac, who refused to accept that he had fathered a daughter despite overwhelming evidence to the contrary, or Ginsberg, whose support for di Prima contrasted strongly with his general view that great art was the product of strong homosocial (and often homosexual) ties between men, and that women tended to be disruptive figures whose presence constantly thwarted the pursuit of art. Di Prima's choice of lifestyle thus signifies not only the ongoing desire to be a non-conformist, but also a challenge to a Beat ideology largely shaped by men.

While Glassman, Jones and di Prima offer various accounts of the difficulties of being a female artist working within the Beat community and of the strategies required to overcome numerous forms of prejudice, it is important to remember that their experiences were not typical of all women whose lives intersected with leading male Beats, and that not all these women would even consider themselves to be 'Beat' (or to be writers) at all. Carolyn Cassady (b. 1923), second wife of Neal Cassady and one of the most tireless champions of Cassady and Kerouac since their deaths in 1968 and 1969, provides a very different account of life as wife to a legendary Beat figure.

Until she met Neal Cassady, Carolyn Robinson seems to have led a relatively conventional life, unmarked by the signs of rebellion and feelings of alienation expressed by women like Hettie Cohen and Diane di Prima. After a childhood spent in Michigan and Nashville, she studied drama and art at Bennington College in Vermont, worked in a fabric company and then served first as an air-raid warden and later as an occupational therapist during the Second World War. After the war, she moved to Denver to study for a master's in fine arts and theatre arts and to work at the Denver Art Museum.

Against many of her own instincts, all of this changed after she met Neal Cassady (as well as Kerouac and Ginsberg) in 1947. Any illusions that Carolyn harboured about the relationship were shattered when she discovered Neal in bed with his first wife and Ginsberg and she moved to San Francisco to live with her sister. Carolyn – or slightly fictionalized versions of her – features heavily in Kerouac's writings about his friendship with Neal in the next few years: Neal found her in San Francisco; they were married and had a baby; he spent their life savings on a down payment on a Hudson and drove off with his first wife to find Kerouac; Carolyn spent much time weeping and despairing about what Neal was doing to her and his indifference to their child; she began an affair with Kerouac (at Neal's suggestion) and Kerouac lived with them while he worked as a brakeman; she had two more children, became a devotee of the celebrity psychic Edgar Cayce (and would do nothing without assessing it in his terms) and eventually divorced Neal in 1963.

And yet, this synopsis – drawn from Kerouac's books – also serves as an illustration of the manner in which Kerouac's own preconceptions could limit his understanding of events and lead him to offer only a partial representation of the people he describes. In particular, his eulogies to Neal in *On the Road* and *Visions of Cody* are often accompanied by unreasonably negative representations of the women who featured in his life and, in particular, of Carolyn. Carolyn Cassady's *Off the Road* (1991) is – as the title suggests – a text self-consciously constructed as a counterpoint to Kerouac's most famous work. Cassady is candid in her admission that, at the time, she had little idea of what Kerouac and Neal did during the lengthy periods when she was left to look after house and children as they travelled the continent. The book's opening chapters offer insights into the chaotic nature of Neal's life, although they also reveal a man who could, in between his bouts of 'madness', be a considerate and loving husband and father. In chapter 30, however, this all changes as Carolyn's role as (in her eyes) the least important member of the triangular relationship with Neal and Kerouac (who was then living in the Cassadys' attic) is replaced by a new order with her at the centre. With Neal working on the railroad and often having to spend days or even weeks away from home, Carolyn was spending much time with Kerouac, although there was no suggestion of a physical relationship. It was only when Neal hinted that this situation should change that Carolyn was able to empower herself when, after initially feeling enormous pain at the idea that her husband would share her with another man, she announced to Neal, 'Let's try it your way.' Carolyn's account of the transformation is worth quoting, since it captures the manner in which her new life is a fruitful fusion of conventional and unconventional behaviour:

> The hope that my gamble would change the pattern of our lives was well founded . . . Now, I was part of all they did; I felt like

the sun of their solar system, all revolved around me. Besides, I was now a real contributor for once; my housework and child-care had a purpose that was needed and appreciated. I was functioning as a female and my men were supportive. It may have taken two of them to complete the role usually filled by one, but the variety was an extra added attraction. They were such different types. How lucky could a girl get?[4]

Cassady seems to achieve what, in her assessment, is the best of both worlds: it is clear that she is happy with the prescribed gender roles of the time, being delighted that she is 'functioning as a female' overseeing the domestic space while the men perform other tasks. And yet, as her willingness to engage in sexual relationships with both men indicates, she is also acting in a way that would shock her neighbours if they knew – a point of which she is aware and which provides a regular source of amusement. The fact that her actions also provoke an element of jealousy in Neal is an added bonus for Carolyn, whose decision to seize the initiative by taking Neal at his word has afforded her a position of both happiness and power.

While *Off the Road* does, therefore, demonstrate the way in which one woman could challenge the behavioural patterns that made Kerouac and Neal Cassady famous and transform her own status from outsider/victim to empowered hub of a three-sided relationship, we need to remember that this transformation did not last. Tensions between the men developed and Kerouac took to living in Skid Row hotels rather than in the Cassadys' attic. In 1954–5, Neal was involved in a love affair with Natalie Jackson, a young friend of Ginsberg, Peter Orlovsky and Robert LaVigne, the artist whose painting of Orlovsky had caught

[4] Carolyn Cassady, *Off the Road: My Years with Kerouac, Cassady and Ginsberg*, extract in *The Portable Beat Reader*, edited by Ann Charters (London: Penguin, 1992), pp. 452, 456.

Ginsberg's eye and led to the start of Ginsberg and Orlovsky's decades-long relationship. Jackson was devoted to Neal to the extent that she forged Carolyn's signature to enable him to withdraw her life savings, which he promptly (and inevitably) gambled away. Always mentally fragile and now overwhelmed with guilt, Jackson descended into an increasingly paranoiac state and committed suicide by slitting her own throat and then slipping through the grasp of a police officer to fall three storeys to her death. While Neal, characteristically, returned to Carolyn and expected her to comfort him in his grief, the incident marked a further deterioration in their relationship.

Subsequently, the success of *On the Road* exacerbated the rift between Kerouac and Neal – who felt that the book made him look foolish and calculating – and, indirectly, led to Neal's imprisonment in San Quentin for selling two sticks of marijuana to an undercover cop. Carolyn did not see Kerouac again after 1960, although she became used to his late-night drunken phone calls and continued to correspond with him regularly. By the early 1960s, she felt that the only way in which she could re-establish any kind of order in her life was by divorcing Neal, although *Off the Road* suggests that, with hindsight, Carolyn regretted the decision and believed that it gave Neal even more freedom to pursue the self-destructive lifestyle that would lead to his early death. The contrasts between their lives in the 1960s indicate why Carolyn's dreams of domestic contentment – whether with one man or two – were ultimately unrealistic. While she returned to child-raising and developed her interests in parapsychology, Neal drove the bus for Ken Kesey's Merry Pranksters, lived with the Grateful Dead and generally performed the role expected of 'Dean Moriarty', although he seemed to tire of the constant attention that he received. After years of frenetic activity often fuelled by speed, he was found dead next to the railroad tracks outside San Miguelle de Allende in Mexico, dressed characteristically (despite the cold, wet weather) only in

T-shirt and jeans, having left a wedding party with the intention of walking to the next town. In *Off the Road*, Carolyn indicates that she was – even then – still willing to take Neal back and had advised him to go to Mexico to sort himself out before he returned to her and the children in California, and her life since then – although now long-domiciled in England – has been largely devoted to championing the lives of the Beat men she knew.

It is striking that – with the exception of di Prima – all the women discussed in this chapter are known largely for their autobiographical reminiscences of their time with Kerouac and the other male Beats, and that their intermittent resurfacings in the mainstream media inevitably focus on these memories. While all have had successful careers and have continued to remain active long after Kerouac, Cassady, Ginsberg, Burroughs and others have died, it seems that even half a century after the publication of *On the Road* they cannot escape its lengthy shadow. Their reception within the post-Beat community is rather different, however: in the 1960s, when feminist politics emerged as much through discontent with the sexism that infused an otherwise increasingly revolutionary counterculture as through rejection of the dominant culture's norms, a later wave of poets such as Anne Waldman – whose first collection of poems, *On the Wing*, was published in 1968 – combined indebtedness to pioneering Beat women with language infused with 1960s radicalism. As the final chapter of this *Beginner's Guide* will show, the sorts of literary genealogy that can be traced through Beat and post-Beat female artists are just one strand in a much wider process of acknowledging and adapting Beat Generation literature that has extended across half a century and around most of the world.

Conclusion: Legacy of the Beat Generation

Travelling in Greece in the summer of 2007, I was struck by a familiar image in an advertisement occupying a half-page in a leading left-leaning newspaper. Although my Greek-language skills are hardly fluent, I was able to work out that the paper was giving away *On the Road* (in translation) as part of a series celebrating the great literary works of the twentieth century. Half a century after its publication, it appears that the Beat Generation's most famous creation is not only more popular than ever, with a global readership and with plans for a movie version directed by Brazilian film-maker Walter Salles (scheduled to be released in 2009), but also is receiving the critical acclaim that was lacking when a conservative literary and cultural establishment did its best to bury the book and its author beneath a mountain of scorn and abuse. In the United States, both the Beat canon and the beatnik caricature have entered the pop-cultural lexicon: *The Simpsons*, perhaps the most acute register of what has been 'in' and 'out' in the popular imagination across the past two decades parodied 'Howl' as a way of articulating Lisa Simpson's angst and alienation in a world without respect for her intellectual ambitions, while, in another episode, do-gooder neighbour Ned Flanders' breakdown is traced back to neglectful beatnik parents. *On the Road* is used to sell jeans and, while Kerouac died almost penniless in 1969, his relatives fought an ill-tempered battle for control of his multi-million-dollar estate and the original scroll manuscript of *On the Road* was sold for US$2.43 million in 2001. Beat Generation works are now taught in most colleges and universities and in many high schools, and – unlike even a decade ago – there is no sense that writing a PhD thesis on Burroughs, Ginsberg or Kerouac will damage the chances of an academic career. City Lights Bookstore has become a landmark on the San Francisco tourist trail and its owner, Lawrence Ferlinghetti, was made Poet Laureate of San Francisco in 1998. In addition, the plethora of academic and media events to mark *On the Road*'s half-century suggest that there is no imminent danger of a waning of interest in the Beat Generation a decade after the deaths of Allen Ginsberg and William Burroughs. While Ginsberg spent much of his life ceaselessly promoting his own and his friends' work, and must indubitably receive much of the credit for bringing it to the public's attention, the Beat Generation are probably more widely known now than at any time, even in their 1950s and early 1960s heyday. While the response to the publication of Amiri Baraka's 9/11 poem, 'Somebody Blew up America', suggests that ex-Beats retain the ability to shock, the overwhelming response to the Beat Generation from academics, marketers and publishers is one of accommodation and – at times – nostalgia for the vanished America that they represent.

What the leading Beats would have made of this is a questionable point. Kerouac and Baraka both (though for different reasons) distanced themselves from the counterculture of the 1960s, which was imagined by others as a rebellious child of rebellious Beat Generation parents. In contrast, many of the other members of the early New York and West Coast Beat scene became pivotal to the next generation's artistic community: Ginsberg served not only as sometime mentor to Bob Dylan but also as a leading figure in areas such as green and anti-nuclear movements, gay rights, and anti-war campaigns, in addition to continuing to produce important and widely read poetry and making regular stage appearances with artists as diverse as Paul McCartney and The Clash. Dylan himself, especially in his early years and in his remarkable renaissance in the new millennium is a fellow traveller, a poet of an America that mixes William Blake with fast cars and motorbikes, Leadbelly with avant-garde art, and bar-room romances between down-on-their-luck wanderers with an unshakable faith in the ability of art to create new worlds.

Likewise, fellow readers at the Six Gallery on the night in October 1955 when Ginsberg first performed 'Howl', were at least as prominent in the 1960s and beyond as they had been in the previous decade: Gary Snyder and Michael McClure, in particular – both of whom featured at San Francisco's 1967 Human Be-In that heralded the city's imminent 'Summer of Love' – brought interests in Eastern philosophy and in environmentalism to a much larger hippie community. McClure was one of several countercultural figures to become friends with the Hell's Angels, working with 'Freewheelin Frank' (Reynolds), the secretary of the San Francisco chapter, on the latter's autobiography (1967) and on efforts to set McClure's poetry to music in the mid-1960s, as well as establishing close links with a new generation of artists such as Jim Morrison and Ray Manzarek of The Doors. Snyder has managed to juggle careers (if this word is appropriate in describing someone who refuses to be contained within conventional boxes) as poet, environmental activist and academic, receiving the prestigious Bollingen Prize for Poetry and the John Hay Award for Nature Writing in 1997, and continuing to be active in the shaping and reshaping of green activism. Diane di Prima, too, bridged the gap between Beat and hippie, and William Burroughs – though his unique brand of subversive dissidence hardly fits the archetype of either 1950s Beat or 1960s countercultural rebel – became not only one of the most popular novelists among young activists but also an idiosyncratic figure present at several key moments in the 1960s' turbulent history. Even Neal Cassady, whose published works are limited to *The First Third* (1971), an autobiographical account of his childhood, and his *Collected Letters* (2004), and who died alone alongside a railroad track in 1968, lives on for new generations of Beat aficionados, not only through their responses to *On the Road*, but also as a heavily mythologized presence driving Ken Kesey's Merry Pranksters' bus, and in the reminiscences of Kesey, Charles Bukowski and many others. A movie, directed by Noah Buschel, chronicling Cassady's life from the publication of *On the Road* until his death was in production in the summer of 2007.

While I suspect that many Beats would have been uncomfortable with the commodification of their work, they would, perhaps, have been happier to see it continue to influence what they would recognize as 'serious' artists. Kerouac's writings have been used to advertise jeans, but have also been featured by the avant-garde poet-musician Patti Smith, who used his words as a springboard into her own improvisations on the tribute CD *Kerouac—Kicks Joy Darkness* (1997), which also features a collection of other Beats and Beat-inspired artists. Tom Waits, the Grateful Dead, Van Morrison and Lucinda Williams openly acknowledge their indebtedness to Beat ideology and lifestyle, while a younger generation of American (and other) musicians continue to celebrate the kinds of kicks experienced by Sal Paradise and Dean Moriarty or lament the passing of a 'golden age' when such kicks were possible.

Although the Beat Generation continues to be identified as an American phenomenon, it is important not to overlook its global dimensions. By this, I do not simply mean the fact that Ginsberg, Orlovsky, Burroughs, Corso, Ferlinghetti and Snyder (to name but a few) spent many years living beyond the North American continent, researching other cultures and incorporating their studies of other literatures and communities within their own work. While a knowledge of this aspect of Beat writing is fundamental to an understanding of the degree to which it revolutionized American literature in its fusion of a national canon of Walt Whitman, Hart Crane, Henry Miller and William Carlos Williams with the literary histories of Europe, China, Japan and South America, it is also essential that we remember the degree to which non-American writers of the same generation were also heavily Beat inflected. For example, in his global travels during the 1960s and 1970s, Allen Ginsberg met with hundreds of 'Beat' writers working within a spectrum of political environments, in countries including Cuba and the Eastern Bloc.

Ironically – given the Beat Generation's own sense of marginalization from mainstream American life – the much-sought copies of *Howl* and *On the Road* that found their way behind the Iron Curtain functioned as a kind of 'soft power' in the Cold War efforts to win over young Eastern minds to the glories of American life. Beat writing and writers could often raise awkward questions for the political leaders of states opposed to America. For example, Ginsberg's leftist politics and faith in the political function of the artist could appeal to senior figures in the Cuban Revolution, yet his homosexuality challenged another, more conservative side of their culture. Likewise, his popularity among the student youth in Prague – which led to his being crowned as May King in 1965 and, swiftly afterward, to his deportation – highlighted the gulf between the desires of an educated, urban community interested in the arts and their Stalinist masters, and foreshadowed the events of the Prague Spring of 1968. By 1990, the underground of the 1960s had become the leaders of a post-Soviet Czech Republic and President Václav Havel (playwright and long-term advocate of avant-garde American art from the Beat Generation to the Velvet Underground) made moves to establish American experimental musician Frank Zappa as a Special Ambassador. In a response aimed at swiftly re-establishing the status quo, then US Secretary of State James Baker let Havel know that he could conduct business with the Beat/hippie America of Zappa or with the United States government, but not with both.

While the Beat Generation occasionally came close to the owners of political power in the communist and post-communist world, their influence on Western Europe tended to be more confined to the arts. Most famously of all, the iconic band of the 1960s, The Beatles, had been renamed from the 'Quarry Men' to the 'Silver Beetles' (a play on 'Buddy Holly and the Crickets') before John Lennon and Stuart Sutcliffe changed 'Beetles' to 'Beatles' in a nod both to the kind of music they were playing and to the American literary influences that were as important to Lennon as they were to Bob Dylan. Paul McCartney became a generous (and usually anonymous) supporter of the London avant-garde art scene of the 1960s in part through his interest in Beat literature and subsequently became a friend of and collaborator with Allen Ginsberg. For the generation of young Britons who had become teenagers in the 1950s, the exotic, romantic landscape portrayed by Jack Kerouac offered a thrilling alternative to a world of rationing and cities still heavily scarred by the German bombs of the Second World War. For The Beatles – and for legions like them – America was largely known through the popular culture of Rock and Roll, 'juvenile delinquent' movies such as *The Wild One*, *The Blackboard Jungle* and *Rebel without a Cause* and the (often hard to obtain) writings of Kerouac, Ginsberg and the other Beats, and the worlds constructed in their works made many young people desperate to travel to the United States.

Ironically, by the time that the United Kingdom was waking up to the Beat Generation, the movement was demonstrably on the wane in the United States. Kerouac, disgusted by what he perceived to be the corruption of his message, had more or less withdrawn from public life and drifted into the chronic alcoholism that would lead to his death in 1969, while Ginsberg, Burroughs and Snyder had spent much of the period since the publication of *Howl* and *On the Road* living outside America. By the mid-1960s, when interest in the Beat Generation probably peaked in the United Kingdom, America was preparing for the Summer of Love and for the New-Left-inspired protests against the Vietnam War which represented a major contrast to the Beat Generation's general desire to distance themselves from direct engagement with political life. This should not, however, lead us to downplay the significance of British Beat poets of the mid-1960s, or of events such as the Albert Hall Incarnation of 1965, which may be viewed retrospectively as a pivotal moment in the decade's countercultural awakening. Thus, while densely populated modern Britain is geographically too small ever to match the United States as a region to be romanticized in the manner achieved by Kerouac, poets such as Michael Horovitz and Tom Raworth redeployed the lessons taught by American Beats in ways that afforded opportunities to challenge a staid poetic establishment and a class system that seemed systematically to discourage challenges to the social and literary orders. Significantly, the Albert Hall Incarnation envisaged poetry as an international form, able to transcend boundaries that would remain intact politically or economically. Thus, the union of British and American Beats envisaged a form of transnationalism that would only become widely embraced thirty or forty years later.

While an international response to the Beat Generation in the 1960s is perhaps unsurprising, I would like to conclude by turning to events from 2007 that illustrate the ongoing international engagement with its legacy. Of course, the year marked the fiftieth anniversary of the publication of *On the Road* and witnessed interviews with most of the surviving Beats in newspapers and on television. It also saw the reissue of seminal Beat narratives, such as Carolyn Cassady's *Off the Road* and the publication of the original scroll manuscript of *On the Road*, which I discuss below. In addition, the *New York Times Book Review* published an illustrated feature by Dwight Garner, featuring reproductions of the front covers of editions of the novel from around the world across the past half-century.[1] More than anything else, this collection of covers helped to explain why *On the Road* – in many ways a quintessentially American text – has become a brand recognized around the world. In almost every instance, whether the cover came from Eastern or Western Europe, Asia or elsewhere, the image seemed to fuse a sense of the potential of the American landscape – that is, the raw materials that had attracted Kerouac in the first place – with something specific to the edition's local/national culture. While it might be possible to offer a depressing interpretation of this pattern as indicative of a wider process of Americanization of global cultures, I think that it suggests something more positive about *On the Road* in particular and Beat Generation ideas more generally. First, it is important to see this kind of reception as part of a circular process within which the Beat Generation – always keen to learn from other cultures – pass their interpretations back to their sources. For example, the reshaping of Eastern philosophies by Beat Generation writers can be regarded as an instance of the borrowings and re-borrowings that have marked global developments in the arts over the past century and more. Second, it appears that Beat notions of freedom, generated specifically to counter the political and psychological repressions that characterized the Cold War America of the 1950s, have resonated with alienated and dispossessed young people who have felt oppressed within their own communities and have responded to the promises of freedom they have identified in Beat literature. While it would be an overstatement

[1] Dwight Garner, 'The Road Goes on Forever', *New York Times Book Review*, 19 August 2007.

to suggest that the Beat Generation tapped into universal human desires (an idea prevalent during the 1950s, but rightly questioned since), it is evident that their texts have provided imitable models of resistance for many dissident individuals and groups and – as the example of the Czech Republic noted above indicates – have contributed to moments of revolution elsewhere that outstrip the changes that they inspired in the United States.

It remains undeniable that, despite the notable achievements of the writers discussed in this book (and many more beside), *On the Road* continues to dominate memories of the Beat Generation. As part of the celebrations of its first half-century, the scroll manuscript has been displayed around the world, although, ironically, one of the consequences of this is to remind us that the original text is actually nearer to sixty than fifty years old. The exhibition has been twinned with Viking Penguin's issue of an expensively produced edition of *On the Road: The Original Scroll*, containing not only Kerouac's text, but also a hundred pages of critical essays, notes, suggestions for further reading and a tentative reconstruction of what the original ending (eaten by Lucien Carr's dog) might have looked like. The beautifully produced book shows just how much interest in the Beat Generation has developed since the days in the early 1950s when their works would most likely be published (if at all) in cheap paperback editions like the Ace Books version of William Burroughs's *Junky*, which first appeared as part of a double package also containing a reprint of a 1941 novel called *Narcotic Agent* by Maurice Helbrant in a series designed to be read and discarded by people riding on the New York subway and never reviewed by literary critics.

Bibliography

This bibliography offers an introduction to primary and secondary works by and about the Beat Generation. It is not intended to be exhaustive, but does provide listings of many of the most important texts. There are numerous editions of the works of Jack Kerouac and several of the other authors included. Editions listed here are those referred to in the text of this book.

Baldwin, James. *Another Country* (London: Black Swan, 1984).

Brautigan, Richard. *A Confederate General from Big Sur* (Edinburgh: Rebel Inc, 1999).

——. *Revenge of the Lawn: Stories 1962–1970* (Edinburgh: Rebel Inc, 1997).

——. *Trout Fishing in America* (London: Vintage, 1997).

Burroughs, William. *The Adding Machine (Collected Essays)* (London: John Calder, 1985).

——. *Junky* (London: Penguin, 1977).

——. *Naked Lunch* (London: Flamingo, 1993).

——. *Queer* (New York: Viking, 1985).

Campbell, James. *Paris Interzone* (London: Secker & Warburg, 1994).

——. *This is the Beat Generation: New York, San Francisco, Paris* (London: Secker & Warburg, 1999).

Cassady, Carolyn. *Off the Road: My Years with Cassady, Kerouac and Ginsberg* (New York: Penguin, 1991; London: Black Spring Press, 2007).

Cassady, Neal. *The First Third: A Partial Autobiography and Other Writings* (San Francisco: City Lights, 1981).

—— *Collected Letters, 1944–1967*, edited by Dave Moore, introduction by Carolyn Cassady (New York: Penguin, 2004).

Caveney, Graham. *The 'Priest' They Called Him: The Life and Legacy of William S. Burroughs* (London: Bloomsbury, 1997).

Charters, Ann. *Kerouac: A Biography* (San Francisco: Straight Arrow, 1973).

—— (ed.). *The Portable Beat Reader* (London: Penguin, 1992).

Chénetier, Marc. *Richard Brautigan* (London: Methuen, 1983).

Cleaver, Eldridge. *Soul on Ice* (London: Panther, 1970).

Cook, Bruce. *The Beat Generation* (New York: Scribner's, 1971).

Corso, Gregory. *Bomb* (San Francisco: City Lights, 1958).

——. *The Vestal Lady on Brattle* (Cambridge, MA: Richard Brukenfeld, 1955).

Couvares, Francis G. (ed.). *Movie Censorship and American Culture* (Washington and London: Smithsonian Institution Press, 1996).

Davidson, Michael. *The San Francisco Renaissance: Poetics and Community at Mid-century* (Cambridge, England: Cambridge University Press, 1989).

Davis, Miles with Quincy Troupe. *Miles: The Autobiography* (London: Picador, 1990).

Di Prima, Diane. *Memoirs of a Beatnik* (London: Marion Boyars, 2002).

——. *Recollections of My Life as a Woman: The New York Years* (New York: Viking Penguin, 2001).

Ellis, R.J. *Liar! Liar!: Jack Kerouac, Novelist* (Billericay, England: Greenwich Exchange, 1999).

Ferlinghetti, Lawrence and Nancy J. Peters. *Literary San Francisco* (New York: Harper & Row, 1980).

Frank, Thomas. *The Conquest of Cool: Business Culture, Counterculture, and the Rise of Hip Consumerism* (Chicago: University of Chicago Press, 1997).

French, Warren. *Jack Kerouac: Novelist of the Beat Generation* (Boston: Twayne, 1986).

Friedan, Betty. *The Feminine Mystique* (London: Penguin, 1992).

Gifford, Barry and Laurence Lee. *Jack's Book* (London: Hamish Hamilton, 1979).

Ginsberg, Allen. *Collected Poems, 1947–1980* (London: Penguin, 1987).

——. *Howl and Other Poems* (San Francisco: City Lights, 1956).

——. *Kaddish and Other Poems* (San Francisco: City Lights, 1961).

——. *Reality Sandwiches* (San Francisco: City Lights, 1963).

Goodman, Paul. *Growing up Absurd: Problems of Youth in the Organized Society* (New York: Vintage Books, 1960).

Greenberg, Clement. 'Avant-Garde and Kitsch', in *Partisan Review*, 6.5 (1939), pp. 34–49.

Halper, Jon (ed.). *Gary Snyder: Dimensions of a Life* (San Francisco: Siera Club Books, 1987).

Harris, Oliver. *William Burroughs and the Secret of Fascination* (Carbondale: Southern Illinois University Press, 2003).

Hipkiss, Robert A. *Jack Kerouac: Prophet of the New Romanticism* (Lawrence, KS: Regent's Press, 1976).

Hoffman, Abbie. *Revolution for the Hell of It* (New York: Dial Press, 1968).

Holmes, John Clellon. *Go* (New York: Thunder's Mouth Press, 1988).

——. *Nothing More to Declare* (London: Andre Deutsch, 1968).

Hunt, Tim. *Kerouac's Crooked Road* (Hamden, CT: Archon Books, 1981).

Johnson, Joyce. *Minor Characters: A Beat Memoir* (New York: Houghton Mifflin, 1983).

Johnson, Roanna C. and Nancy M. Grace (eds.). *Girls Who Wore Black: Women Writing the Beat Generation* (New Brunswick, NJ and London: Rutgers University Press, 2002).

Jones, Hettie (Hettie Cohen). *How I Became Hettie Jones* (New York: Dutton, 1990).

Jones, LeRoi. *Blues People: The Negro Experience in White America and the Music that Developed from It* (New York: William Morrow, 1963).

Kerouac, Jack. 'About the Beat Generation', in *The Portable Jack Kerouac*, edited by Ann Charters (New York: Penguin, 1996).

——. *Beat Generation* (Richmond, England: Oneworld Classics, 2007).

——. *Big Sur* (London: Panther, 1980).

——. *Desolation Angels* (St Albans, England: Granada, 1982).

——. *The Dharma Bums* (St Albans, England: Granada, 1982).

——. *Doctor Sax* (London: Panther, 1984).

——. *Lonesome Traveller* (St Albans, England: Granada, 1982).

——. *Maggie Cassidy* (St Albans, England: Granada, 1982).

——. *On the Road* (London: Penguin, 1972).

——. *On the Road: The Original Scroll* (London: Penguin, 2007).

—— *Orpheus Emerged* (New York: Ibooks, 2002).

——. *The Portable Jack Kerouac*, edited by Ann Charters (New York: Penguin, 1996).

——. *The Subterraneans* (New York: Grove Press, 1971).

——. *The Town and the City* (New York: Harcourt, Brace, 1950).

——. *Vanity of Duluoz* (St Albans, England: Granada, 1982).

——. *Visions of Gerard* (New York: McGraw-Hill, 1976).

Kesey, Ken. *One Flew over the Cuckoo's Nest* (London: Picador, 1973).

Krim, Seymour. *Shake It for the World* (London: Allison & Busby, 1971).

MacAdams, Lewis. *Birth of the Cool: Beat, Bebop and the American Avant-Garde* (London: Scribner's, 2002).

McClure, Michael. *Scratching the Beat Surface* (San Francisco: North Point Press, 1982).

Mailer, Norman. 'The White Negro', in *Advertisements for Myself* (London: Panther, 1970).

Marcuse, Herbert. *One-Dimensional Man* (London: Ark, 1986).

Miles, Barry. *Allen Ginsberg: A Biography* (London: Virgin, 2002).

——. *The Beat Hotel: Ginsberg, Burroughs and Corso in Paris, 1957–1963* (London: Atlantic Books, 2001).

——. *Jack Kerouac, King of the Beats: A Portrait* (London: Virgin, 1998).

——. *William Burroughs: El Hombre Invisible* (London: Virgin, 1992).

Mottram, Eric. *William Burroughs: The Algebra of Need* (London: Marion Boyars, 1977).

Nicosia, Gerald. *Memory Babe: a Critical Biography of Jack Kerouac* (New York: Grove, 1983).

Panish, Jon. *The Color of Jazz: Race and Representation in Postwar American Culture* (Jackson: University Press of Mississippi, 1997).

Peabody, Richard (ed.). *A Different Beat: Writings by Women of the Beat Generation* (London: Serpent's Tail, 1997).

Plummer, William. *The Holy Goof: A Biography of Neal Cassady* (Englewood Cliffs, NJ: Prentice-Hall, 1981).

Podhoretz, Norman. 'The Know-Nothing Bohemians', in *Doings and Undoings* (London: Rupert Hart-Davis, 1965).

Rexroth, Kenneth. *American Poetry in the Twentieth Century* (New York: Herder & Herder, 1971).

Riesman, David, with Nathan Glazer and Ruel Denney. *The Lonely Crowd: A Study of the Changing American Character* (New Haven: Yale University Press, 1950).

Rosenberg, Harold. 'The American Action Painters', in *The Tradition of the New* (London: Thames & Hudson, 1962).

Roszak, Theodore. *The Making of a Counter Culture: Reflections on the Technocratic Society and Its Youthful Opposition* (Berkeley: University of California Press, 1995).

Skerl, Jennie. *William S. Burroughs* (Boston: Twayne, 1985).

Southern, Terry. *Now Dig This: The Unspeakable Writings of Terry Southern, 1950–1995* (London: Methuen, 2002).

Stephenson, Gregory. *The Daybreak Boys: Essays on the Literature of the Beat Generation* (Carbondale: Southern Illinois University Press, 1990).

Townsend, Peter. *Jazz in American Culture* (Edinburgh: Edinburgh University Press, 2000).

Tytell, John. *Naked Angels: The Lives and Literature of the Beat Generation* (New York: McGraw-Hill, 1976).

Weinreich, Regina. *The Spontaneous Poetics of Jack Kerouac* (Carbondale: Southern Illinois University Press, 1987).

Whaley, Preston, Jr. *Blows Like a Horn: Beat Writing, Jazz, Style, and Markets in the Transformation of U.S. Culture* (Cambridge, MA and London: Harvard University Press, 2004).

Whyte, William H. *The Organization Man* (New York: Simon & Schuster, 1956).

Index